PICTURE YOURSELF
Making
Jewelry and Beading

Step-by-Step Instructions and Inspiration for Creating
Unique, Handmade Jewelry

Denise Etchison and Sandy Doell

ISBN-10: 1-59863-450-X

ISBN-13: 978-1-59863-450-1

Library of Congress Catalog Card Number: 2007938241

Printed in the United States of America

08 09 10 11 12 BU 10 9 8 7 6 5 4 3 2 1

Publisher and General Manager, Thomson Course Technology PTR:
Stacy L. Hiquet

Associate Director of Marketing:
Sarah Panella

Manager of Editorial Services:
Heather Talbot

Marketing Manager:
Jordan Casey

Acquisitions Editor:
Mitzi Koontz

PTR Editorial Services Coordinator:
Erin Johnson

Copy Editor:
Heather Kaufman Urschel

Interior Layout:
Shawn Morningstar

Cover Designer:
Mike Tanamachi

Cover Photographs:
Diane Howard Photography and
T.H. Blevins Photography

Interior Photographs:
Diane Howard and
T.H. Blevins Photography

Indexer:
Broccoli Information Management

Proofreader:
Melba Hopper

Thomson Course Technology PTR,
a division of Thomson Learning Inc.
25 Thomson Place
Boston, MA 02210
http://www.courseptr.com

Sandy: For my son, Bruce Boshears.
You see the art in everything.

Denise: For my daughter, Calee Etchison.
I love you more than all the points on all the stars.

Acknowledgments

DENISE WOULD LIKE TO THANK her many friends and family for their patience, encouragement, support, and love. Rex, Dianna, Dan, Michele, Brandon, Dustin, Lucas, and Calee, thank you for all the extras.

I feel blessed to have been given this opportunity to work with such a wonderful, hardworking group: Sandy Doell, Diane Howard, and Mitzi Koontz, and all the others responsible for the publishing of this book.

A very special thanks to the following talented instructors, mentors, and friends:

Sally J. Phillips, my kidnapped gypsy friend

Kim Kniest of Nimblerods.com for your friendship and artistic talent

Kendra Roberts of MYKSJ.com for sharing your extraordinary talent

My "1979" people

Thank you to the following: Laura Villanyi of LAURA-WORLD.com beads, BeadforLife.org, and Art in Hand Co-op Gallery

Thanks to everyone at the Indianapolis Art Center, and special thanks to:

Melanie Reckas of Basile Studio Gift Shop

Annie Minnich-Beck, Associate Director of Education

T.H. Blevins Photography

Diane Howard Photography

Rachael Schatko and Ingrid Craft of raku beads coalcreekclay@sbcglobal.com

Heidi Hale of Heidi J. Hale jewelry.com

Sonya Rhivera

Thanks to everyone who was able to participate in the studio workshops and everyone who answered my questionnaires as I did research for this book. And thank you to my many friends and mentors, who are too many in number to mention individually, but I express my heartfelt thanks to you all.

SANDY WOULD LIKE TO THANK Mitzi Koontz for inspiring her to undertake just one more project and for bringing together a great team of enthusiastic professionals; Heather Kaufman Urschel for her excellent copy editing, Photoshop suggestions, and enthusiastic cheerleading; Shawn Morningstar for once again rallying to do the impossible and to do it on deadline; Mike Tanamachi for working his cover art magic to bring together the art forms represented here (jewelry design, photography, writing, and book design) to create a cover that is a snapshot of all that is inside the book; Jordan Casey, who has a way with words and people (a rare combination); Melba Hopper, who inspires the best in us all with her generosity of spirit, unflagging energy, and love for her fellow human beings, as well as her talent with the English language (and border collie language); Kevin Broccoli and Broccoli Information Management for a job cheerfully well done; and finally, thank you to Denise Etchison, who actually is the sole author of this book. I was just her interpreter.

Thank you, once again, to my patient family and friends, who graciously postponed many things while I became obsessed with my work yet again.

About the Authors

DENISE ETCHISON was raised on a farm in central Indiana, where she always felt an urge to make art. She spent many hours walking the corn rows searching for what some might call ordinary rocks, but she called her "treasures." With a little care and polish, she knew their beauty could be brought out. Early attempts at artwork were created from old fence wire and barn roofing found on the farm.

Until 1996, Denise spent most of her professional life working in retail and merchandising while raising her daughter Calee. Then, by chance, she drove past the Indianapolis Art Center and saw a sign that said "Register Now for Classes." Over the next few years, she embarked on an artistic exploration that took her from ceramics and steel sculpture and finally to her true passion—jewelry design. She was fortunate enough to find encouraging teachers to mentor her in wire wrapping, glass fusing, metalsmithing, and stone inlay, all of these forming the foundation of her training in jewelry fabrication. Lapidary work (the cutting and shaping of stones) and the creation of silver settings (*bezels*) to place stones in has become her favorite form of design. It allows her to return to the earlier joy she found in collecting rocks and fossils, letting their naturally occurring patterns and geometry inspire her creations.

In 2000, Denise began to give back to the community that encouraged her skills by becoming a jewelry instructor at the Indianapolis Art Center. She built her own home studio in 2003, where she teaches private lessons and workshops. She began to sell her artwork through retail venues and at art fairs. Through teaching and participation in art fairs, Denise has been able to add the element of human interaction so important to inspiring a creative life. Denise loves seeing her students' eyes light up when they master a new skill or when speaking to someone who has found inspiration and joy in wearing her jewelry designs.

SANDY DOELL has worked in the publishing industry as an editor and writer for over 15 years. She has edited hundreds of books and is the author of *Picture Yourself Planning Your Perfect Wedding* and the co-author of *Picture Yourself Decorating Cakes*, both published by Thomson/Course Technology PTR. Her first book, *Mom's Field Guide: What You Need to Know to Make It Through Your Loved One's Military Deployment*, published in 2006 by Warrior Angel Press, is based on her experiences when her son, David, was deployed to Iraq with the U.S. Army in 2004.

Table of Contents

Introduction

TODAY'S TREND TO MAKE IT YOURSELF, the awakening of the pioneer spirit, the desire to make something yourself and then wear it with pride is never more evident than in the artistic community. Handmade jewelry is a favorite at art fairs and galleries, and here you will learn the skills and techniques necessary to DIY (do it yourself) for fun, pleasure, profit, and pride in your own abilities. You'll love to wear the jewelry you learn to make on the following pages, and giving these pieces as gifts, knowing that a part of you went into making them, is one of the more rewarding experiences you'll have in life. You do not have to be a professional with a dedicated studio of your own and lots of money invested to make the jewelry we teach you to make here.

After you've done a couple of these projects, though, you may just find yourself setting aside a room, a work table, or some space in your home dedicated to your creations and searching for beads and metal of all types and colors to add to your cache of materials. Everyone is creative; sometimes we just need a little advice and experience to express that creativity. You'll find the advice you need to gain some useful jewelry design experience in *Picture Yourself Making Jewelry and Beading.*

What You'll Find in This Book

WITH MORE THAN A DOZEN different projects, and variations on many of them, you'll find much here to pique your interest and inspire your creativity. Hundreds of photographs illustrate every step necessary to create these one-of-a-kind works of art so that you can learn every technique and skill required to create your own jewelry. All you need is inspiration, and you'll find lots of that here too—from the unique and beautiful handmade beads used in Chapter 1, "Working with Wire and Beads," to the BeadforLife beads used in Chapter 3, "Modern Chandelier Earrings," right through to Hippie Queen Necklace, the last project in Chapter 12, "Fun Variations—Combining Components." Along the way, you will learn the basics of creating your own jewelry, including how to work with jump rings, why you should always wear safety glasses, where to find inexpensive "practice" materials, and more.

Simple detailed step-by-step instructions from an experienced instructor, enable you to jump in at any point in the book and complete a project. You can start at the beginning and work your way through as the projects go from very simple to more elaborate, or depending on your level of expertise, you can jump in at any point.

Mostly, what you'll find here is inspiration to have fun and indulge your creative side. Your goal as a jewelry artist, above all, should be to have fun and enjoy making these projects and many more that you will design yourself.

Picture Yourself Making Jewelry and Beading includes projects that require limited tools and encourage the use of inexpensive alternative materials. You are encouraged to improvise with what you have on hand or what is easily obtained. You will learn to think outside the box and see many uses for ordinary items and to check out your garage or workroom before you go shopping for expensive tools.

The materials we use in the book are inexpensive. Ordering them is simple and easy, and we point you toward some of our favorites in the Resources Appendix. Using the techniques demonstrated in this book, you will be able to create many very different types of jewelry from just a few simple materials.

Neither will the projects featured in *Picture Yourself Making Jewelry and Beading* require a lot of expensive tools. Most of the tools used are readily available at your local hardware or home improvement stores. The projects you learn in this book will give you the skills and ideas you need to go on and create your own personal designs.

Who This Book Is For

THE JEWELRY PROJECTS FEATURED in this book are meant to inspire students at every level of expertise. Beginning jewelry artists will be able to expand on the basics. They will find useful tips and information about the basic tools required for jewelry making and instruction in the basic techniques that are to be mastered as they move through the stages of learning.

Experienced artists will find new design ideas that will, in turn, inspire them to create their own even more unique designs. Experienced jewelry designers will find ideas and techniques that they can incorporate into their own designs along with new ideas for combining various components. The options here will spark your imagination to create endless variations on the designs we present. You may also learn some new techniques to incorporate into your current designs.

We encourage you to experiment and to go beyond the projects we present here. If you have an idea, get to work on it. If it doesn't work, well, mistakes are part of the learning process, and often, a mistake leads to a new idea for a completely new design. There is no such thing as wasted time doing art of any kind. As you work on these pieces, you will gain the confidence to experiment. There is no wrong. The more you experiment, the more options you will have with your designs. At the very least, as you experiment you will learn what doesn't work!

There is always something new to learn. Jewelry making is a constant learning process with no end in sight!

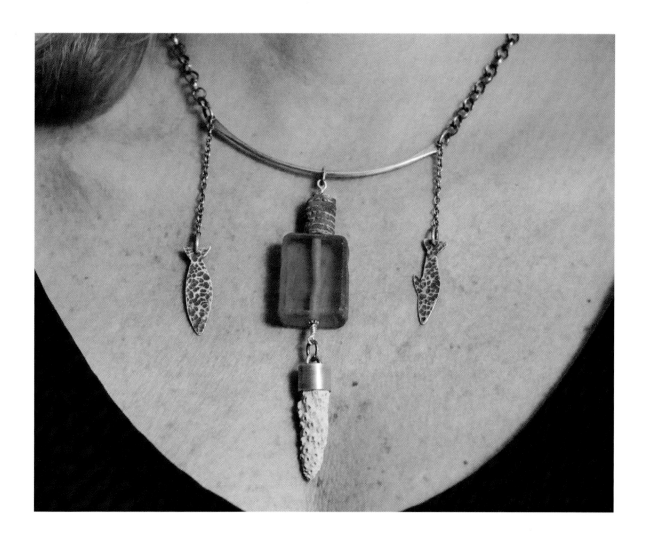

Tools You Will Need

IN THE LISTS OF TOOLS required for the projects in this book, you will often find a choice of tools or instructions on how to "make do" with what's available. Don't have a rawhide mallet? A piece of scrap leather and a regular hammer will easily do the same job without the need to invest in an expensive specialized tool.

Jewelry projects can require many, often expensive, tools. Before you decide to invest in expensive specialty tools, which you may only occasionally use, raid the garage workbench, toolbox, junk drawers, local hardware stores, auctions, garage sales, antique shops, and flea markets. Learn to adapt and make do with what's available.

Jewelry supply catalogs are always full of great tips and suggestions on the items and products that they carry. Subscribe to as many as possible and study them often. Look for items that serve multiple purposes:

- ☐ Wooden dowel rods, PVC pipe, or old wooden baseball bats can be used to shape wire and sheet silver.
- ☐ Pencils, pens, markers, or bamboo skewers can be used to make jump rings and coil beads.
- ☐ Use a concrete block or garden pavers to texture sheet silver.
- ☐ A regular inexpensive hammer, used carefully, can be used to texture sheet silver.
- ☐ Screwdrivers and nail set punches can be used to stamp sheet silver.

- ☐ Inexpensive wire from your local hardware store or home improvement center can be used to experiment with designs before committing to more expensive sterling silver or gold.
- ☐ Cover metal with a thick piece of scrap leather on a hard flat surface and gently hammer it to flatten the metal.

Always think "outside the box" when you are looking for tools. They do not have to be expensive and you can accumulate them over time as you find yourself needing something specific to a certain job.

Here's a list of things you'll find a need for as you work through the projects in this book. Most are fairly inexpensive.

- ☐ **Pliers**: Many specialty pliers are available through jewelry supply companies. Before you invest in more costly specialty pliers, start with just the basic necessities: two pairs of chain nose pliers, two pairs of round nose pliers, and a good pair of cutters. You can start out with low cost pliers, decide what you use most and start to upgrade your pliers as needed. Always keep a good pair close at hand to use for many tasks.
- ☐ **Round nose pliers**: Round smooth tapered jaws. Used to make loops and curved bends in wire and metal. Can purchase at local arts and crafts store or through a jewelry supply company.

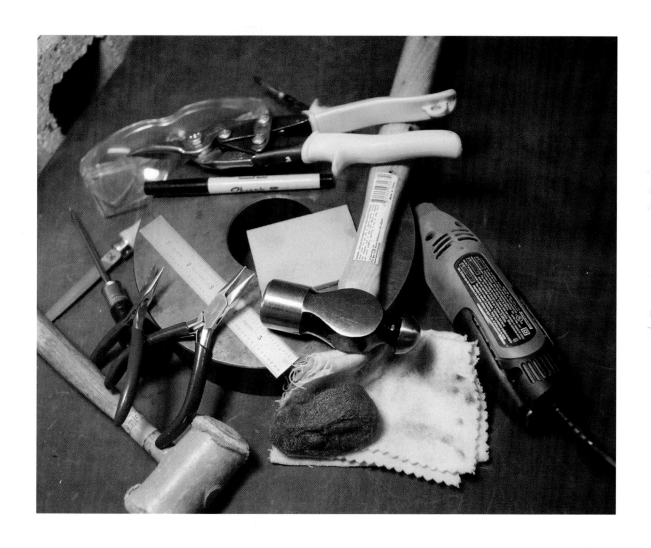

Chain nose pliers: Flat, smooth, tapered jaws. Used to grip small components and to bend and shape wire and metal. It's good to have at least two pairs available. Can purchase at local arts and crafts store or through a jewelry supply company.

Black Permanent Marker: Black...yes; blue...no. Use a permanent black marker as a guide for cutting and measuring. Blue permanent marker will stain some stones and beads and will not come off. Marks from a black permanent marker can be removed from a metal surface using fine steel wool. Both fine and ultra fine markers are good to have. Buy them by the boxful from office supply stores.

Ruler: Metal is best; the measurements are more accurate. You can find good ones at any jewelry supply company or office supply store.

Hard flat surface: This is a smooth steel surface. Check your local hardware store, metal machine shops, and recycling center for a suitable surface. You can also find this item through jewelry supply companies.

File: You will use files a lot. Some are quite costly but worth the investment if you need them for specific purposes; you can also pick up less expensive ones at the hardware store. Many great files are available through jewelry supply companies. They come in many varieties of coarseness. You may want to purchase an inexpensive set of files and use them until you determine what coarseness will best suit the materials that works best for your needs.

Safety glasses: Not very stylish but absolutely necessary! Make it a habit to wear safety glasses. Unexpected flying metal when you are cutting and long wire flipping around when you're bending it can lead to serious eye injuries. Don't risk it.

Sanding pads: Sanding paper and sanding pads are useful to remove rough edges. Super fine grit is great to use after you've filed metal to smooth the edges and remove file marks. Sanding pads and paper can be cut into any desired size. They are flexible and will fit into small areas. Sanding paper can be used to eliminate small surface scratches on some metal surfaces. Available in wide assortment of grits. Can be used wet or dry.

Hammer: Many specialty hammers are available through jewelry supply companies. Before you invest in costly hammers, start with the basics. A simple ball-peen hammer, flat on one end and rounded on the other purchased from the hardware store, is all you will need to begin. Buy a couple of inexpensive ones and use them until you determine whether you need to invest in a better, more expensive hammer. Once you have a hammer, designate it for jewelry only, taking care that it doesn't find its way in to your garage!

Tin snips: The preferred method to cut sheet silver is to use a jeweler's saw (available through jewelry supply companies), but if you are just starting out and don't want to make that kind of purchase just yet, you can use tin snips. They are great for cutting thick materials. They have a slightly serrated blade, which will leave marks on the cut material. You can eliminate the serrated marks by filing the cut edges of the metal and then sanding them smooth.

Masking tape: Great for many uses. Use masking tape to hold small items in place, to mark items, and to wrap the jaws of your pliers to prevent marring the metal. Use the best quality masking tape you can find. The back of less expensive, lower quality, masking tape is a little too gooey, and it leaves a residue on surfaces.

- **Nail set punch**: Usually come in sets of three sizes. This can be purchased at your local hardware store or home improvement center. Great to stamp circle shapes into metal.

- **Awl**: A pointed tool used to make pilot holes in pieces to be drilled. You can use a small nail instead, but you will need to replace the nail often because the end will quickly become misshapen.

- **1/16" drill bit**: Many bits are available through jewelry supply companies. These can be purchased at your local hardware store or home improvement center. 18-gauge wire and 18-gauge jump rings will fit through the hole created using a 1/16" drill bit.

- **Handheld rotary tool**: A wide variety of brands, styles, and price ranges are available. A handheld variable speed rotary tool serves many uses: polishing, drilling, etching, and more. They usually come with a kit of attachments. Many bits and attachments are available through jewelry supply companies.

- **Liver of sulfur or oxidizing solution**: I recommend purchasing chemicals through a jewelry supply company. They are very knowledgeable about the products and will provide information to you about the product. The company will also provide free Material Safety Data Sheets (MSDS). Always follow the manufacturer's safety recommendations when working with any type of chemical.

- **Fine steel wool**: Use to remove darkened areas on the surface of silver after applying oxidizing solution. Comes in many grades. Rinse your work after using steel wool.

- **Polishing cloth**: Many choices available. Some are treated with rouge for cleaning and polishing.

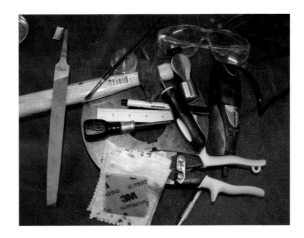

Working with Wire and Beads

Handmade Bead Drop Earrings

Follow the step-by-step instructions to make these basic bead earrings using a loop closure.

MATERIALS NEEDED

Two 1½" head pins (base metal)
Assorted beads
Two sterling silver ear wires

TOOLS NEEDED

Ruler
Marker
Wire cutters or tin snips
Chain nose pliers
Round nose pliers

1. Slide the beads onto the head pin.

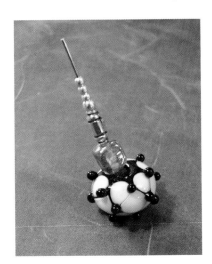

2. Use the ruler to measure and mark ⁵⁄₁₆"
   above the top bead on the head pin. With
   the wire cutters or tin snips, cut the head
   pin wire ⁵⁄₁₆" above the top bead.

3. Using the chain nose pliers, bend the head pin wire next to the top bead at a 90-degree (or right) angle.

4. Hold the head pin with the beads on it in one hand with the wire that you bent pointing toward you. Using the round nose pliers, grip the end of the head pin wire that is pointing toward you, and roll it away from you. Your hand position will be similar to that of holding a bicycle handlebar (think of turning the ignition key to start your car). Release the pliers from the head pin wire. At this point, the opening in the loop at the top of the head pin wire should still be large enough to slip the ear wire on. After adding the ear wire, use the round nose pliers to grasp the loop of the head pin wire and roll the loop closed. If necessary, you can use the round nose or chain nose pliers to adjust the shape of your loop at the top of the head pin.

5. Repeat Steps 1 through 4 for the second earring.

The more you practice this technique, the easier it will become to keep the loop round in shape. As an alternative to using a ruler to measure the spot to cut off the head pin at $\frac{5}{16}$" above the beads, you can designate a bead that is $\frac{5}{16}$" long or a piece of hollow tube cut to $\frac{5}{16}$" long as your measuring rod. Then simply slide the bead or tube onto the top of the head pin and cut the wire directly above it. This will create a uniform length on all of these that you do.

Head pins are available in a wide variety of styles and lengths. They can be found in flat, rounded, balled, paddle, and fancy with a wide assortment of shapes and designs on the ends. You can also find head pins with gemstones and crystals on the ends. Head pins come in many materials: sterling silver, base metal, nickel, 14kt gold, gold-filled, vermeil, and more. Sizes range from $\frac{1}{2}$" to 4".

I use base metal head pins for strength on projects that use a loop closure at the top. Base metal is stronger than sterling silver, and you will not need to worry about the loop coming open. I do use sterling silver for the ear wires; some people are sensitive to base metal because of the nickel content when it comes in direct contact with their skin.

What advice would you offer a beginning artist?

Find an art form that excites you and then find someone competent in that art form to get you started and guide you.

—J. D. Nolan
Traditional Black and White Photography

Handmade Bead Drop Necklace

Follow the step-by-step instructions here to make this basic bead necklace using a loop closure.

MATERIALS NEEDED

One 1½" head pin (base metal)
Assorted beads
One sterling silver jump ring (pictured is round
16-gauge 5 mm × 3.2 mm)
Sterling silver chain with clasp

TOOLS NEEDED

Ruler
Marker
Wire cutters or tin snips
Two pairs of chain nose pliers
Round nose pliers

1. Slide the beads onto the head pin.

2. Use the ruler to measure and mark ⁵⁄₁₆"
   above the top bead on the head pin. With
   the wire cutters or tin snips, cut the head
   pin wire ⁵⁄₁₆" above the top bead.

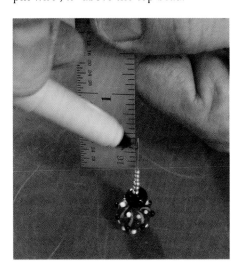

3. Using the chain nose pliers, bend the head pin wire next to the top bead at a 90-degree angle.

4. Hold the head pin with the beads on it in one hand with the wire that you bent pointing toward you. Using the round nose pliers, grip the end of the head pin wire that is pointing toward you and roll it away from you. Again, your hand position will be similar to that of holding a bicycle. Release the pliers from the head pin wire. Use the round nose pliers to grasp the loop of the head pin wire and roll the loop closed. If necessary, you can use the round nose or chain nose pliers to adjust the shape of your loop at the top of the head pin.

5. Open the jump ring and place it through the closed loop at the top of the head pin. Close the jump ring.

To open and close jump rings: With two pairs of chain nose pliers pointing up, hold the jump ring with the opening at the top. Roll one of your wrists away from you and your other wrist toward you, opening the jump ring only as much as necessary to fit it through the loop. To close the jump ring, hold it the same way as you did to open it and roll your wrists in the opposite direction. Think of holding a piece of paper and tearing it. Never pull the jump ring ends straight out; this will weaken the metal, and it will be difficult to close the jump ring.

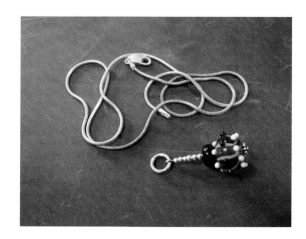

6. Slide jump ring onto the chain and you are done!

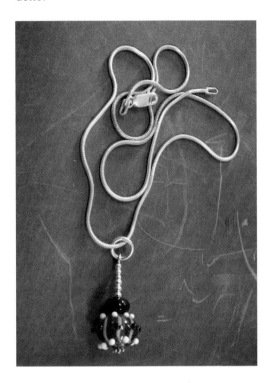

What advice would you offer a beginning artist?

"Follow your passion. It is God-given."

—T.H. Blevins, Photographer

You can make several of these in different colors and styles; they can be interchanged on a chain, ribbon, or leather cord.

Handmade Gypsy Inspired Necklace

This dynamic bead necklace has a lot going on. The use of multiple beads of various sizes on multiple strands of chain brings to mind a twirling gypsy dance. This "gypsy" necklace is made using techniques described in the earring and necklace projects. It can be made using any number of beads and head pins, but using an odd number of beads will help it to hang more evenly when you wear it.

MATERIALS NEEDED

Head pins (1 ½" base metal)
(22 were used for this project)
Assorted beads
18" sterling silver link chain with clasp
9" sterling silver link chain
Two sterling silver jump rings (16-gauge round
5 mm × 3.2 mm were used for the necklace shown)

TOOLS NEEDED

Ruler
Marker
Wire cutters or tin snips
Round nose pliers
Chain nose pliers—2 pair

It's helpful to use a nonslip surface or bead tray to keep your beads from rolling around. This type of surface also comes in handy to lay out your beads and check placement of the various colors before you start to work.

For this project, I used 22 main beads (15 on the bottom strand and 7 on the upper strand) with various accent beads. I used handmade LAURA-WORLD beads that are one of a kind. You can choose similar beads and work to duplicate the pictured necklace or use your favorite beads and color combinations to create your own work of art.

1. Slide the beads onto the head pins.

Slide all of the beads onto the head pins and then lay them out around the chain on a nonslip surface such as a rubber drawer liner to make sure that you like the look of the necklace before you begin to attach them to the chain.

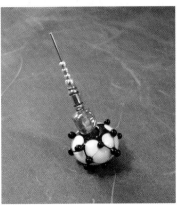

2. Use the ruler to measure and mark ⁵/₁₆" above the top bead on your head pins. With wire cutters or tin snips, cut the head pin wire ⁵/₁₆" above the top bead.

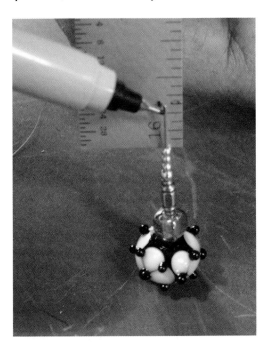

3. Use the chain nose pliers to bend the head pin wire next to the top bead at a 90-degree angle.

4. Hold the head pin with the beads on it in one hand with the wire that you bent pointing toward you. Using the round nose pliers, grip the end of the head pin wire that is pointing toward you and roll it away from you, making sure that the opening in the loop of the head pin is still large enough to slip onto a link of the 18" chain. After you add the head pin to the link of the chain, use the round nose pliers to grasp the loop of the head pin wire and roll the loop closed (I start at the center and work out to each side). To evenly space the beads on the chain, simply count the links of chain between where the head pins are connected. Repeat these steps until you have the desired amount of head pins with beads added to the chain. You will now have a finished 18" single strand necklace.

To make a double-strand necklace, continue with the following steps.

5. Attach the beaded head pins to links of the additional 9" of chain. Lay out the completed single strand necklace with the clasp closed, and then lay out the additional length of chain to determine its placement.

6. Opening and closing jump rings: With two pairs of chain nose pliers pointing up, hold the jump ring with the opening at the top. Roll one of your wrists away from you and your other wrist toward you. Open the jump ring only as much as needed. To close the jump ring, hold it the same way and roll your wrists in the opposite direction. Think of holding a piece of paper and tearing it! Never pull the jump ring ends out; this will weaken the metal, and it will be difficult to close the jump ring.

7. Open one jump ring and slide it through the end loop of the additional 9" chain and then through a link of the necklace. Close the jump ring. Repeat on the other side with the second jump ring.

The necklace pictured is made primarily from LAURA-WORLD™ handmade glass beads.

This necklace is an excellent way to use beads that are left from your other projects. Use any color or bead combination that appeals to you. You can also use charms alternately with your beads to create a different look.

Check with your local art center to see if classes in bead making are offered. Many local bead shops offer classes on bead making. Strike up a conversation with a bead artist at a local art fair; sometimes you can get them to give private instruction. Finally, there are bead societies and clubs throughout the country that offer lots of information on where to get started making beads.

"Be an artist everyday, unique, complex, one of a kind."

By Laura Villanyi, handmade glass bead artist

Basics of making glass beads:

Take a rod of glass and gradually introduce it to a 1500-degree flame that is oxygen and propane fed.

Heat the desired amount of glass until it is molten and then transfer it onto a specially coated stainless steel rod.

While continuously turning it, form the molten glass into a round ball shape.

At this point, you have made a basic bead, but this is also the point where changing the shape or layering color and texture make the bead truly your own.

Still turning the rod, take the glass out of the heat and let it slowly cool down until the glass is no longer moving. Place the bead into an annealing kiln at 950 degrees and let the kiln slowly reduce in temperature for eight hours until the bead is cool enough to remove from the rod and clean.

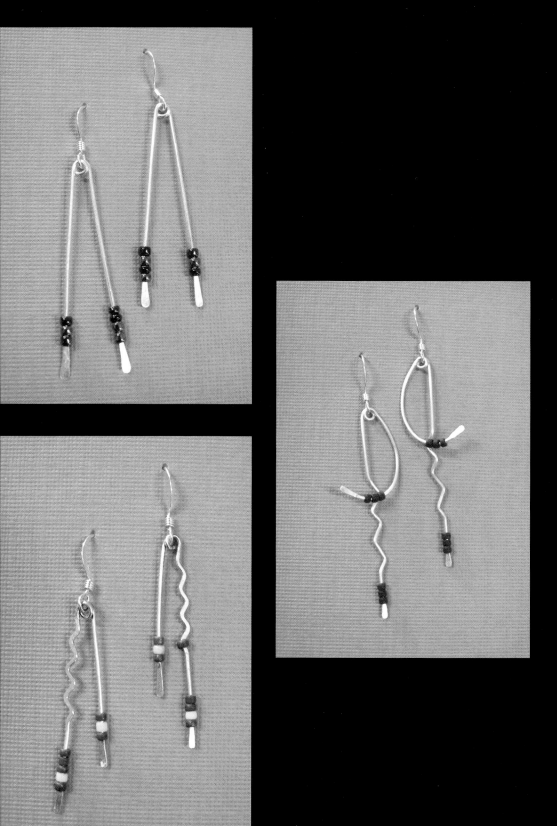

Dancing
Wire
Earrings

Wire and Seed Bead Earrings

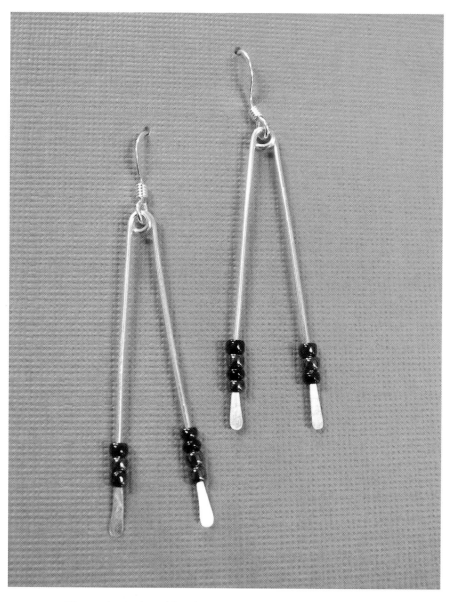

These wire and seed bead earrings are easy and fun to make.
You can let your creativity run free in choosing color combinations and wire configurations.

MATERIALS NEEDED

20-gauge sterling silver wire, approx 7"
Seed beads
Two sterling silver ear wires

TOOLS NEEDED

Ruler
Marker
Wire cutters or tin snips
Round nose pliers
Safety glasses
Hard flat surface
Hammer
File
Fine grit sanding pad
Chain nose pliers

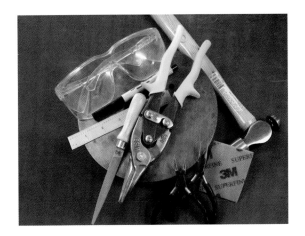

1. You will need two 3½" pieces of 20-gauge sterling silver wire. Use the ruler to measure and mark the 7" piece of 20-gauge sterling silver wire in the center or at 3½". Use the wire cutters or tins to cut the wire.

2. Use the ruler to measure each wire and mark it at 1¾". This is where you will make the loops to attach the ear wire to each earring. By measuring and marking both wires in the same place in this manner, you will be able to keep the loop placement alike on both of the earrings.

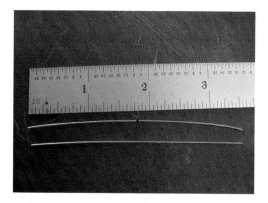

3. Working with one wire at a time, grasp the wire in the jaws of the round nose pliers where you have measured and marked the wire. Hold the wire approximately ⅛" from the tip of the pliers. The closer you hold the wire to the end of the jaws of the pliers, the smaller the loop will be. The further up in the jaws of the pliers you hold the wire, the larger the loop will be.

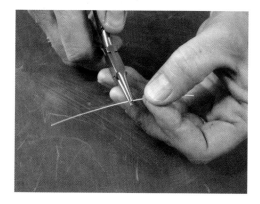

4. Hold the wire firmly in the jaws of the round nose pliers and use your fingers to bend the wire down to form an upside-down U. It will resemble the shape at the top of a bobby pin.

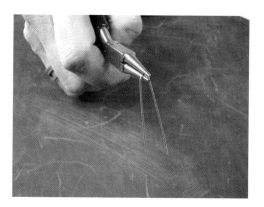

5. Continue to firmly hold the wire in the jaws of the round nose pliers and use your fingers to bend the wire around the pliers until the wire ends are both pointing up. This will form the loop where you will attach the ear wires.

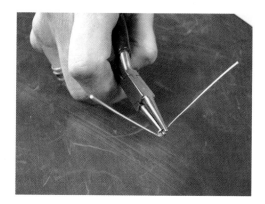

6. Repeat Steps 3–5 with the second wire. Compare the length of the two wires. If necessary, use the wire cutters or tin snips to trim the ends to make them even.

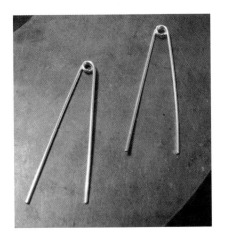

7. Use the ruler to measure and mark the wire ¼" from each end. This will give you a visual guide as you flatten the ends of the wires with the hammer. Flattening the wire ends will keep your seed beads from sliding off.

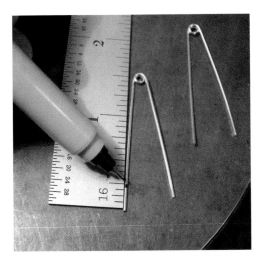

8. Add seed beads to one side of the wire. Slide the seed beads up to the top of the wire next to the loop. This will help to keep them safely out of the way while you are hammering the ends of the wire flat.

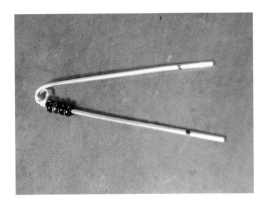

9. Lay the wire on a hard flat surface and, with the hammer, strike the end of the wire with a firm tap using the ¼" mark that you made on the end of the wire as a visual guide. You may need to strike the wire end multiple times to achieve the flatness that you desire. Because this project uses 20-gauge sterling silver wire, you will not need to use a lot of force to flatten the end. It is better to gently strike the end multiple times than to use a lot of force when you strike the wire and risk ruining or misshaping the wire.

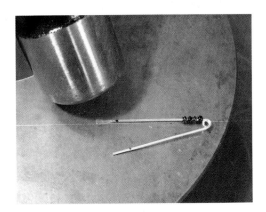

10. Repeat Steps 7, 8, and 9 on each of the wire ends: adding beads, sliding them up to the loop, and then hammering the ends flat on each of the wires. Repeat this process on the other earring.

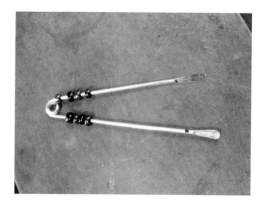

11. File the flattened ends of the wires to remove any sharp or rough edges. Use a fine grit sanding pad to go over the area where you have filed to smooth the edges and remove any file marks. If needed, use the fine grit sanding pad to remove any marker lines on the silver wire.

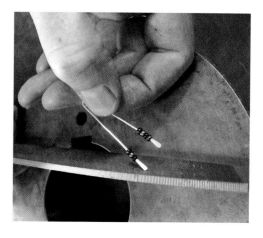

12. With chain nose pliers, gently open the loop at the bottom of the ear wire and place it through the loop that you formed at the top of the beaded wires. Close the loop at the bottom of the ear wire. Repeat this step on the other earring.

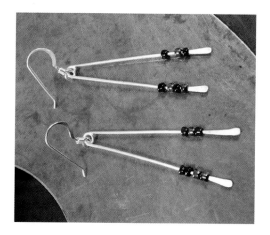

Some of the many variations on this project are pictured here. The possibilities are endless. You can bend zigzags in the wire or curve one end of the wire. If you do choose to add curves and zigzags, you should add enough extra length to the wire so that the earrings still have enough length to dance around your ears.

> **You can pick up inexpensive 20-gauge metal wire at a hardware store and play with your designs before doing them in sterling silver.**

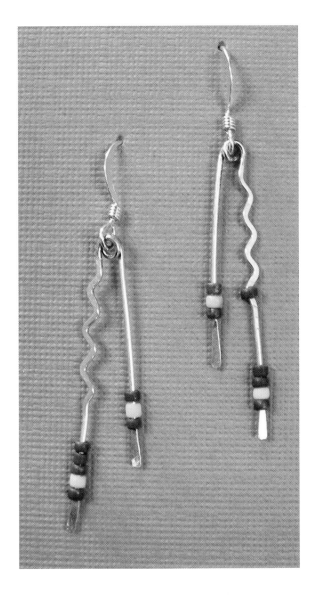

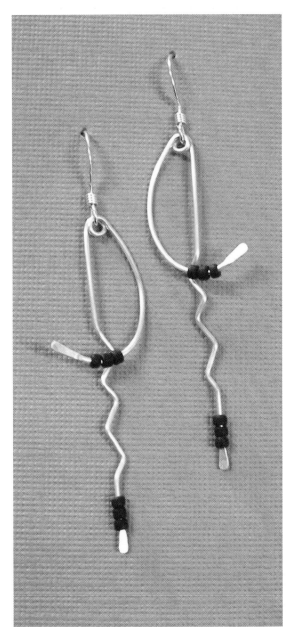

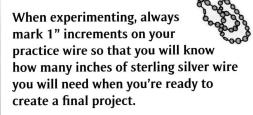

When experimenting, always mark 1" increments on your practice wire so that you will know how many inches of sterling silver wire you will need when you're ready to create a final project.

Modern Chandelier Earrings

Easy Memory Wire and Bead Earrings

Follow these step-by-step instructions to make these easy memory wire chandelier earrings.
These earrings have great movement and mobility; you'll love making them and wearing them.

MATERIALS NEEDED

Bracelet size memory wire (one coil)
Six 1½" head pins (base metal)
Six Bead for Life beads
Two sterling silver ear wires

TOOLS NEEDED

Ruler
Marker
Chain nose pliers
Round nose pliers
Wire cutters or tin snips

When working with memory wire, do not use wire cutters. Instead, use chain nose or flat nose pliers to bend the wire back and forth to break it. It only requires a couple of bends to do this, and it will save your cutters from getting gouges in the blades.

1. Use the ruler to measure and mark the memory wire to approximately 2¼" in length (this is approximately one-half the circumference of the memory wire coil). Break two pieces of the memory wire to identical sizes.

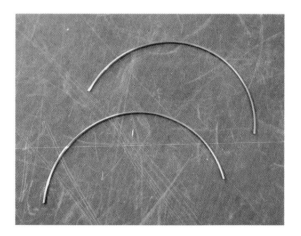

2. Mark the two pieces of memory wire in identical places. This is where you will form the loops to attach the ear wires. You can measure and mark the wires in the center or you can mark them slightly off center, to add interest to your earrings.

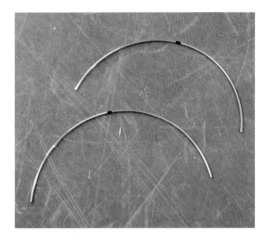

3. Use the round nose pliers to grasp the memory wire where you have made the mark. Hold the wire approximately ⅛" from the end of the tip of the round nose pliers with the wire curving down. This will give you a good size loop through which you can place the eye pin and ear wire.

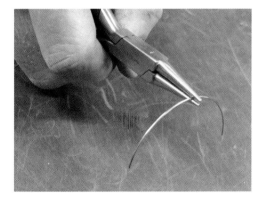

The memory wire is very strong and is designed to keep its round shape, so it is not easily bent.

4. Hold the wire firmly in the jaws of the round nose pliers. Use your fingers to bend the sides of the wire down to form a fish shape.

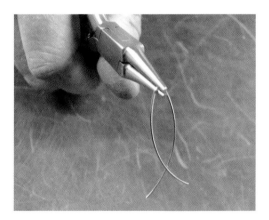

What advice would you offer a beginning artist?

"I don't think you'll ever be rich as an artist, but you will be one of the few who loves their job. You will be rich in your heart and soul."

—Kim Kniest, Metal Art

5. Continue to firmly hold the wire in the jaws of the round nose pliers and, using your fingers, further bend the wire around the pliers until the wire ends are both curved up. This will form the loop where you will attach the ear wires. Continue to bend the memory wire until you have the curve that you want for your earrings. The earrings shown here have a curve that is almost a half circle.

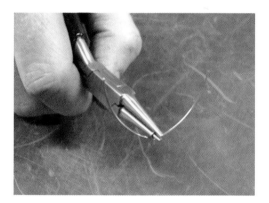

6. Repeat this step with the other wire. After you have bent both wires, you can compare the curve of the two wires and the length of the end wires. Adjust the curves by bending the wires with your fingers. Use the chain nose pliers to break the ends of the memory wire to make the two wires the same length. Remember: Break the memory wire, do not cut it with wire cutters.

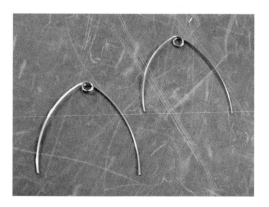

7. To make the loops at the bottom of the curved memory wire, use the round nose pliers to grip the end of the memory wire and roll it inward to form a loop. Release the wire and roll again to close the loop. This wire is not easy to bend, so it may take a few attempts to get the loop closed. Repeat this step on each end of the curved wires. Set these aside.

8. Slide a bead onto a head pin.

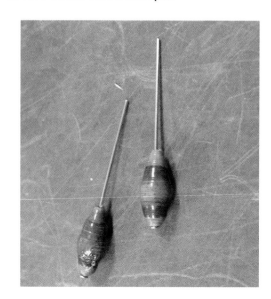

9. Use the ruler to measure and mark $\frac{5}{16}$" above the top of the bead on the head pin. Use the wire cutters or tin snips to cut the head pin wire where you marked.

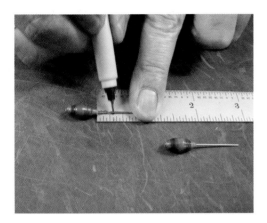

10. Using the chain nose pliers, bend the head pin wire next to the top bead at a right angle.

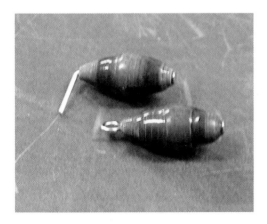

11. Hold the head pin with the bead on it in one hand with the wire that you bent pointing toward you. Use the round nose pliers to grip the end of the head pin that is pointing toward you and roll it away from you. Release the pliers from the head pin. At this point, the opening in the loop at the top of the head pin wire should be large enough to slip onto the loop of the memory wire. After adding the memory wire loop through the head pin loop, use the round nose pliers to grasp the loop of the head pin wire and roll it closed.

12. Repeat Steps 8 through 11 until you have all six of the beaded head pins added to the curved memory wire.

13. Using the chain nose pliers, gently open the loop at the bottom of the ear wire. Slide the center loop of the curved memory wire onto the ear wire and then close the loop of the ear wire.

14. Repeat these steps for the second earring.

You can experiment with different lengths of wire and mix up your bead sizes. You can add length to the earring by using an eye pin or bar component between the ear wire and the center loop of the curved memory wire.

The beads used to create the earrings in this chapter were purchased from BeadforLife. These beautiful beads are made from colorful scraps of paper by Ugandan women. This project, featured on Oprah, NBC News, and in many magazines, is a wonderful effort to partner with hard-working Ugandans to lift their families out of extreme poverty.

The beads themselves are inexpensive and beautiful. BeadforLife also sells finished pieces on their web site, www.BeadforLife.org. Visit the web site—buy the beads. It is a great way to help people leave extreme poverty behind.

"If eyes were made for seeing, then Beauty is its own excuse for being."

—Ralph Waldo Emerson

Wire-Wrapped Cuff Bracelet

Wire-wrapped Sterling Silver Cuff Bracelet

This is a beautiful piece for any age—and very simple to make.

MATERIALS NEEDED

24" 18-gauge sterling silver wire
Pre-made sterling silver cuff bracelet
(You can make your own cuff bracelet from heavy
gauge sterling silver rectangle wire if you prefer.)

TOOLS NEEDED

Liver of sulfur or oxidizing solution
Ruler
Marker
Round nose pliers
Wire cutters or tin snips
File
Chain nose pliers
Fine steel wool
Polishing cloth
Safety glasses

1. Apply liver of sulfur or oxidizing solution to
   the 24" of 18-gauge sterling silver wire.

It is *very* important to follow
any safety recommendations
the manufacturer suggests on the
directions when working with any
chemicals. You will use the fine steel
wool on the oxidized wire to remove
some of the darkened areas after you
complete the wrapping process.

2. Use the ruler to measure and mark the 24" of 18-gauge wire into four sections. Measure and mark the wire at 7", 12", and 17".

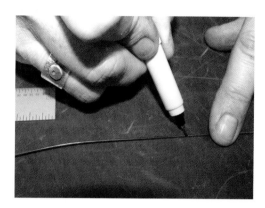

3. Next, measure and mark the center of the top of the cuff bracelet (because it's curved, you can just kind of eyeball it). Then use the ruler to measure and mark ¾" from the center of the cuff to each side.

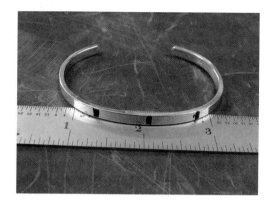

4. Firmly grasp the marked center of the 24" 18-gauge wire in the jaws of the round nose pliers. Use your fingers to bend the sides down to form an upside-down U shape (the wire will resemble a large bobby pin).

When working with long pieces of wire, safety glasses are recommended.

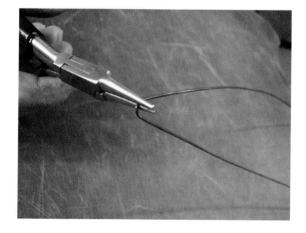

5. Slide the wire onto the sterling silver cuff bracelet to the center mark. Pinch the wire tight onto the cuff bracelet and, while holding the wire on the cuff with your fingers, wrap one side of the wire randomly toward the ¾" mark that you made on the top of the cuff bracelet. You will want to watch where the 7" and the 17" marks are on the wire and use them to match up with the ¾" mark that you made on the cuff bracelet.

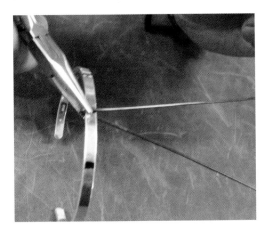

6. Finish wrapping the wire on the other side, matching up the 7" and the 17" marks on the cuff bracelet with the ¾" marks on the 18-gauge wire.

7. Now wrap the wire on one side back toward the center of the cuff bracelet. Then wrap the wire on the other side of the cuff bracelet back toward the center. You may need to trim and file the ends of the wire so that they end up on the backside of the cuff bracelet.

8. Use the round nose pliers to curl the ends of the wire up into the wrapped wire on the underside of the cuff bracelet. Use the chain nose pliers to firmly squeeze the ends up into the other wrapped wire. This will keep the ends securely in place.

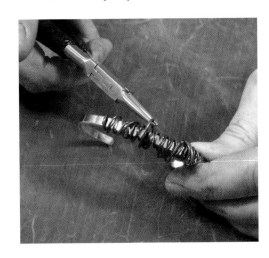

9. Use fine steel wool to remove the darkened area on the surface of the wire, leaving the areas in the crevices of the wrapped wire dark. Buff the wrapped wire and the cuff bracelet with a polishing cloth.

What advice would you offer a beginning artist?

A portrait teacher once told me that by the 500th portrait I would be really good. Lesson—practice; practice every day.

Stick with one medium and do it really well. Craftsmanship is key.

—Laura Villanyi
Flameworking

This cuff is great for men as well as women. Use the larger men's size of pre-made cuff bracelet and add extra length to the 18-gauge sterling silver wire, generally six to eight inches to accommodate the larger men's cuff bracelet.

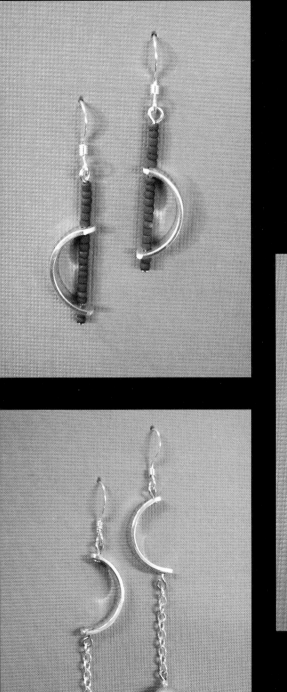

Sterling Silver Crescent and Bead Earrings

Sterling Silver Rectangle Wire and Seed Bead Earrings

Follow the step-by-step instructions to make these basic bead earrings using a loop closure.

MATERIALS NEEDED

Two 1" pieces of 4 × 1 mm sterling silver
    rectangle wire
Two ½" head pins
40 seed beads (approximate number)
Two sterling silver ear wires

TOOLS NEEDED

Ruler
Marker
Jeweler's saw or tin snips
Safety glasses
Hard, flat surface
Awl
Hammer
$\frac{1}{16}$" drill bit
Hand held rotary tool, flex shaft, or drill press
File
Fine grit sanding pad
Ring mandrel
Rawhide mallet
Two pairs of chain nose pliers
Wire cutters or tin snips
Round nose pliers

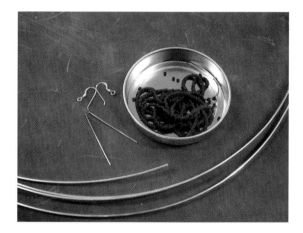

1. Use the ruler to measure and mark two 1"
   pieces of 4 × 1 mm rectangle sterling silver
   wire.

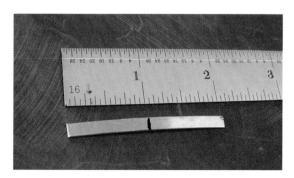

2. Using a jeweler's saw or tin snips, cut the 4 × 1 mm rectangle sterling silver wire into two 1" lengths.

3. File each end of the 1" rectangle wire pieces to remove any burs or rough edges. If desired, you can use the file to round the ends of the rectangle wire pieces. Use a fine grit sanding pad to go over the area where you have filed to smooth the edges and remove any file marks.

4. Use the ruler to measure and mark $\frac{1}{16}$" from each end of the 1" pieces of rectangle wire and place a mark in the center of the wire. This will be where you will drill the holes to slide the head pins through.

5. Put on your safety glasses! Place the 1" rectangle wire pieces onto a hard, flat surface. Place the point of the awl on the mark that you made $\frac{1}{16}$" from each end of the rectangle wire, and firmly strike once on the top of the awl with a hammer. This will make a pilot hole for drilling holes into the rectangle wire.

Always wear your safety glasses when doing any job that might result in metal, stone, or any hard material flying around. Protect your eyes from injury at all times!

If you don't have an awl, you can use a small nail to start your pilot hole. Use the same technique described here for using an awl.

8. Curve both 1" pieces of the rectangle wire into a "C" shape using a ring mandrel and rawhide mallet. Align the holes that you drilled on each end of the 1" rectangle wire pieces. Compare both of the C-shaped rectangle wire pieces and adjust the curves so that they are similar in size.

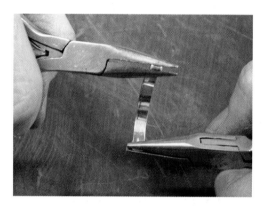

6. Using a 1/16" drill bit, drill holes into each end of the rectangle wire pieces with a handheld rotary tool, flex shaft, or drill press (don't forget to wear your safety glasses!).

7. Use the file or fine grit sanding pad to eliminate any burs or rough edges left from drilling holes into the rectangle wire pieces.

If you do not have a ring mandrel and rawhide mallet, use two pairs of chain nose pliers: Holding one pair in each hand, grasp each end of the 1" rectangle wire piece in the chain nose pliers and gently bend the rectangle wire into a "C" shape.

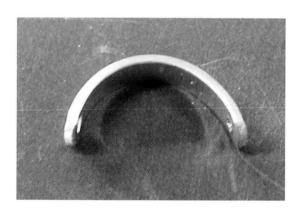

9. Slide the head pin through the holes in the C-shaped rectangle wire to make sure that the holes are vertically aligned and that the head pin slides through both holes easily. Perform these steps for both C-shaped rectangle wires.

10. After testing that the head pins slide easily through the holes in the C-shaped rectangle wire, remove the head pins and set the "C" shapes aside. Add two seed beads to the bottom of the head pin.

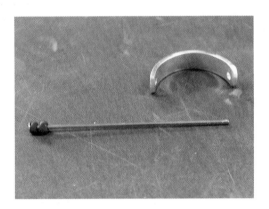

11. Slide the head pin with the two seed beads on it through the bottom hole of the C-shaped rectangle wire.

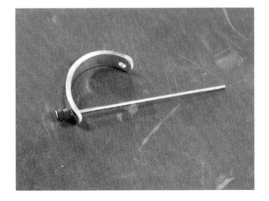

12. Slide seed beads onto the head pin above the bottom hole of the C-shaped rectangle wire. (I used 11 seed beads, but you can adjust the amount of beads that you use. You may need to use more or less beads depending on the size of the beads used and the distance between the holes on the C-shaped rectangle wire.)

13. Slide the head pin through the top hole of the C-shaped rectangle wire.

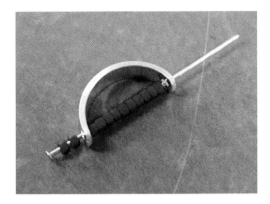

14. Add seed beads to the head pin above the top hole of the C-shaped rectangle wire. I used six seed beads, but, again, you can adjust the amount of beads you use. Just make sure to leave at least $\frac{5}{16}$" of head pin wire above the top seed bead to allow enough wire to make the loop closure.

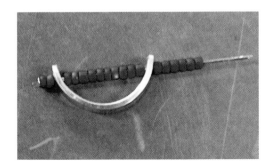

15. Use the ruler to measure and mark ⁵⁄₁₆"
    above the top bead on the head pin. With
    the wire cutters or tin snips, cut the head
    pin wire ⁵⁄₁₆" above the top bead.

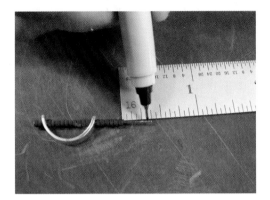

16. Use the chain nose pliers to bend the head
    pin wire next to the top bead at a 90-degree
    angle.

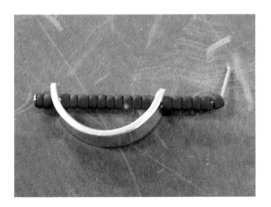

17. Hold the head pin with the beads and the
    rectangle wire on it in one hand with the
    wire that you bent pointing toward you.
    Using the round nose pliers, grip the end of
    the head pin wire that is pointing toward
    you and roll it away from you (your hand
    position will be similar to that of holding a
    bicycle handlebar). Release the pliers from
    the head pin wire. At this point, the opening
    in the loop at the top of the head pin wire
    should still be large enough to slip the ear
    wire on. After adding the ear wire, use the
    round nose pliers to grasp the loop of the
    head pin wire and roll it closed. If necessary,
    you can use the round nose or chain nose
    pliers to adjust the shape of the loop at the
    top of the head pin.

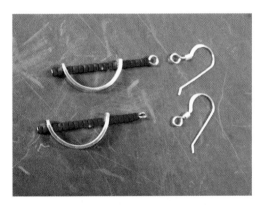

18. Repeat these steps for the second earring.

Sterling Silver Rectangle Wire, Hollow Rubber Tube, and Turquoise Earrings

MATERIALS NEEDED

3" 4 × 1 mm sterling silver rectangle wire
Twenty-one ½" head pins
Two turquoise disc beads
One ½" 1.7 mm black hollow rubber tube
Two sterling silver ear wires

TOOLS NEEDED

Ruler
Marker
Jeweler's saw or tin snips
Safety glasses
Hard, flat surface
Awl
Hammer
$\frac{1}{16}$" drill bit
Hand held rotary tool, flex shaft, or drill press
File
Fine grit sanding pad
Ring mandrel
Rawhide mallet
Two pairs of chain nose pliers
Scissors
Wire cutters or tin snips
Round nose pliers

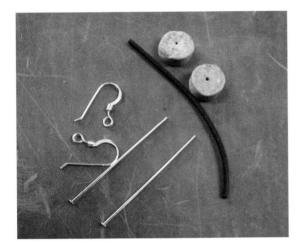

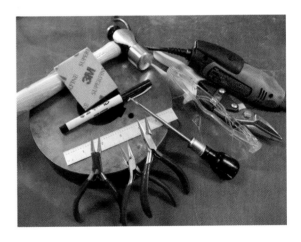

What advice would you offer a beginning artist?

"Do what you love. Explore different media. Sell on a selective, limited, basis at first to see what works or what doesn't work for you before you jump into a major outlay of money and effort."

—Sally J. Phillips, Jewelry Designer

1. Use the ruler to measure and mark two 1½"
   pieces of 4 × 1 mm rectangle sterling silver
   wire.

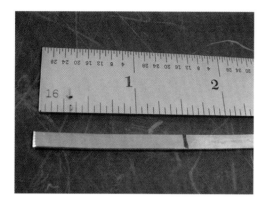

2. Using a jeweler's saw or tin snips, cut the
   4 × 1 mm rectangle sterling silver wire into
   two 1½" lengths.

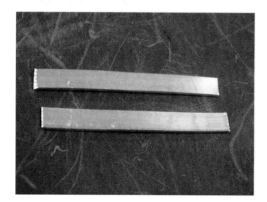

3. File each end of the 1½" rectangle wire
   pieces to remove any burs or rough edges.
   If desired, you can use the file to round the
   ends of the rectangle wire pieces. Use a fine
   grit sanding pad to go over the area where
   you have filed to smooth the edges and
   remove any file marks.

4. Use the ruler to measure and mark ⅟₁₆" from
   one end of the 1½" pieces of rectangle wire
   and place a mark in the center of the wire.
   This is where you will drill the holes to slide
   the head pins through.

5. Put on your safety glasses!!! Place the 1½"
   rectangle wire pieces onto a hard, flat surface. Place the point of the awl on the mark
   that you made ⅟₁₆" from one end of the
   rectangle wire pieces, and firmly strike once
   on the top of the awl with a hammer. This
   will make a pilot hole for drilling holes into
   the rectangle wire.

6. Using a $\frac{1}{16}$" drill bit, drill holes into one end of the rectangle wire pieces with a handheld rotary tool, flex shaft, or drill press (while still wearing your safety glasses!).

7. Use the file or fine grit sanding pad to eliminate any burs or rough edges left from drilling holes into the rectangle wire pieces.

8. Curve both 1½" pieces of rectangle wire into a "C" shape using a ring mandrel and rawhide mallet. If you do not have a ring mandrel and rawhide mallet, use two pair of chain nose pliers. Holding one pair of pliers in each hand, grasp each end of the 1½" rectangle wire piece with the pliers and gently bend the rectangle wire into a "C" shape. Compare both of the C-shaped rectangle wire pieces and adjust the curves so that they are similar in size. Set these aside.

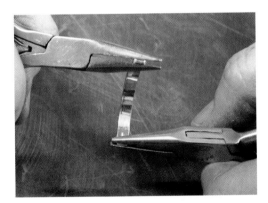

9. Use the ruler to measure and mark the rubber tube into four equal pieces measuring $\frac{3}{8}$" each. Use scissors to cut the rubber tube.

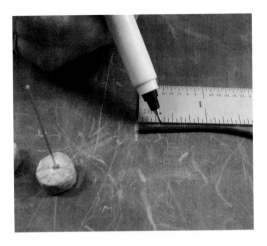

10. Place the turquoise disc bead onto the head pin and add one $\frac{3}{8}$" piece of the rubber tube, place the head pin through the hole in the C-shaped rectangle wire, and then add the other $\frac{3}{8}$" piece of rubber tube.

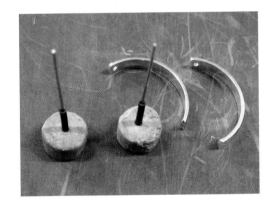

11. Use the ruler to measure and mark ⁵⁄₁₆"
above the top piece of the hollow rubber
tube. With the wire cutters or tin snips, cut
the head pin wire ⁵⁄₁₆" above the top of the
hollow rubber tube.

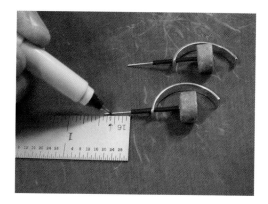

12. Use the chain nose pliers to bend the head
pin wire next to the top of the rubber tube
at a 90-degree angle.

13. Hold the head pin with the bead, rubber
tube, and the rectangle wire on it in one
hand with the wire that you bent pointing
toward you. Using the round nose pliers, grip
the end of the head pin wire that is pointing
toward you and roll it away from you (think
of turning the ignition key to start your car).
Release the pliers from the head pin wire.
At this point, the opening in the loop at the
top of the head pin wire should still be large
enough to slip the ear wire on. After you add
the ear wire, use the round nose pliers to
grasp the loop of the head pin wire and roll
it closed. You can use the round nose or
chain nose pliers to adjust the shape of the
loop at the top of the head pin if you need to.

14. Repeat these steps for the second earring.

Sterling Silver Rectangle Wire, Pearl, and Chain Earrings

MATERIALS NEEDED

Six 1½" head pins
2" 4 × 1 mm sterling silver rectangle wire
Two 1" pieces of sterling silver chain
Two pearl beads
Two 1.4 mm round sterling silver beads
Two sterling silver ear wires

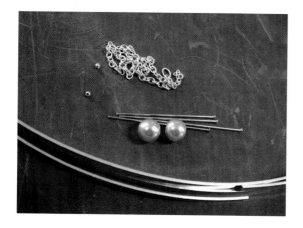

TOOLS NEEDED

Ruler
Marker
Jeweler's saw or tin snips
Safety glasses
Hard, flat surface
Awl
Hammer
1/16" drill bit
Handheld rotary tool, flex shaft, or drill press
File
Fine grit sanding pad
Ring mandrel
Rawhide mallet
Two pairs of chain nose pliers
Wire cutters or tin snips
Round nose pliers

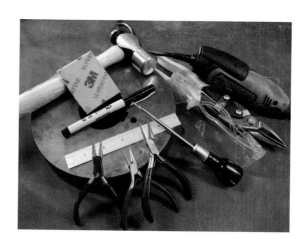

What advice would you offer a beginning artist?

Just enjoy doing it. You'll make a lot of bad art along with the good—but the good is worth it!

—Lynne Miller, Ceramics Artist

1. Use the ruler to measure and mark two 1" pieces of 4 × 1 mm rectangle sterling silver wire.

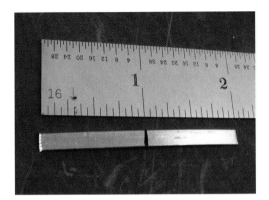

2. Using a jeweler's saw or tin snips, cut the 4 × 1 mm rectangle sterling silver wire into two 1" lengths.

3. File each end of the 1" rectangle wire pieces to remove any burs or rough edges; you can use the file to round the ends of the rectangle wire pieces if you want. Use a fine grit sanding pad to go over the area where you have filed to smooth the edges and remove any file marks.

4. Use the ruler to measure and mark 1/16" from each end of the 1" pieces of rectangle wire and place a mark in the center of the wire. This will be where you drill the holes to slide the head pins through.

5. Next, put on your safety glasses! Then place the 1" rectangle wire pieces onto a hard, flat surface. Place the point of the awl on the mark that you made 1/16" from each end of the rectangle wire pieces, and use a hammer to firmly strike once on the top of the awl. This will make a pilot hole for drilling holes into the rectangle wire.

8. Curve both 1" pieces of rectangle wire into a shape using a ring mandrel and rawhide mallet. If you do not have a ring mandrel and rawhide mallet, use two pairs of chain nose pliers. Holding one pair in each hand, grasp each end of the 1" rectangle wire piece in the chain nose pliers and gently bend the rectangle wire into a "C" shape, aligning the holes that you drilled on each end of the 1" rectangle wire pieces. Compare both of the C-shaped rectangle wire pieces and adjust the curves so that they are similar in size. Set these aside.

6. Using a 1/16" drill bit, drill holes into each end of the rectangle wire pieces with a handheld rotary tool, flex shaft, or drill press (while still wearing your safety glasses!).

7. Use the file or fine grit sanding pad to eliminate any burs or rough edges left from drilling holes into the rectangle wire pieces.

9. Use the ruler to measure the chain into 1" pieces. Use the wire cutters to cut the chain, and set these pieces aside.

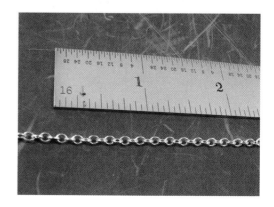

10. Place a head pin through a pearl bead and then add one 1.4 mm sterling silver bead.

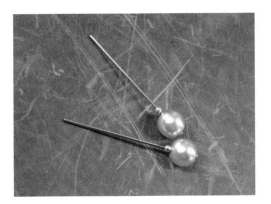

11. Use the ruler to measure and mark $\frac{5}{16}$" above the top bead on the head pin. With wire cutters or tin snips, cut the head pin wire $\frac{5}{16}$" above the top bead.

12. Using the chain nose pliers, bend the head pin wire next to the top bead at a 90-degree angle.

13. Hold the head pin with the pearl bead and the silver bead on it in one hand with the wire that you bent pointing toward you. Using the round nose pliers, grip the end of the head pin wire that is pointing toward you and roll it away from you (think of turning the ignition key to start your car). Release the pliers from the head pin wire. At this point, the opening in the loop at the top of the head pin wire should be large enough to slip the 1" length of chain on it before closing the loop of the head pin. After you add the chain, use the round nose pliers to grasp the loop of the head pin wire and roll it closed. You can use the round nose or chain nose pliers to adjust the shape of the loop at the top of the head pin if you need to.

14. Repeat this step on the second pearl and silver bead. Set these aside.

15. Place a head pin through the hole drilled into one end of the rectangle wire "C" shape with the bottom or flat end on the inside curve of the rectangle wire "C" shape. Use the ruler to measure and mark the head pin $\frac{5}{16}$" above the rectangle wire. With wire cutters or tin snips, cut the head pin wire $\frac{5}{16}$" above the top of the rectangle wire.

16. Use the chain nose pliers to bend the head pin wire next to the rectangle wire at a 90-degree angle.

17. With the chain nose pliers in one hand, hold the bottom or flat area of the head pin firmly against the rectangle wire with the head pin wire that you bent pointing toward you. With your other hand, use the round nose pliers to grip the end of the head pin wire and roll it away from you. Release the head pin wire. At this point, the opening in the loop of the head pin wire should still be large enough to slip the end link of the 1" chain onto it. Now add the chain to the loop of the head pin, and then use the round nose pliers to grasp the loop of the head pin wire and roll it closed. You can use the round nose or chain nose pliers to adjust the shape of the loop at the top of the head pin.

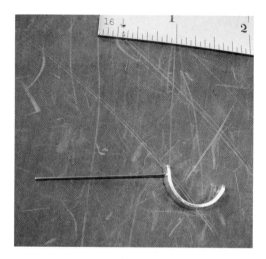

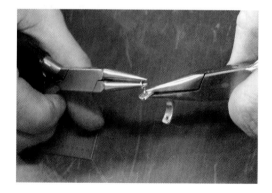

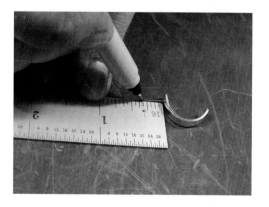

18. Repeat this process on the other hole in the C-shaped rectangle wire. Instead of adding the 1" length of chain with the pearl and the sterling silver bead, add the ear wire at the other end. Slip the ear wire onto the loop of the head pin before closing the loop.

19. Repeat the preceding steps on the second earring.

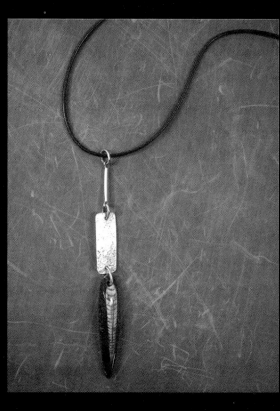

Ancient Elements Textured Silver Earrings, Bracelet, and Necklace

Ancient Elements Textured Silver Earrings

These rustic-looking pieces get their texture from a cement block!

MATERIALS NEEDED

Two ½" × 1" 18-gauge sterling silver sheet silver
Two ⅞" sterling silver bar components
Two 5.3 mm × 3.2 mm 16-gauge sterling silver
      oval jump rings
Two sterling silver ear wires

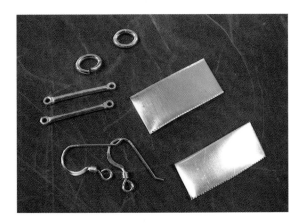

TOOLS NEEDED

Ruler
Marker
Jeweler's saw or tin snips
Masking tape
Concrete block or landscape paver
Hammer
File
Fine grit sanding pad
Awl
Hard, flat surface
$\frac{1}{16}$" drill bit
Handheld rotary tool, flex shaft, or drill press
Liver of sulfur or oxidizing solution
Fine steel wool
Polishing cloth
Two pairs of chain nose pliers

1. Use the ruler to measure and mark two ½" × 1" rectangle pieces of 18-gauge sterling sheet silver.

2. Using a jeweler's saw or tin snips, cut the 18-gauge sterling sheet silver into two ½" × 1" rectangles (if you will be making the bracelet and pendant projects, you may want to cut all of the rectangle silver pieces needed for the other projects and texture them all at one time).

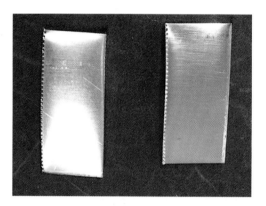

3. Place the two ½" × 1" sterling silver rectangle pieces onto the sticky side of a piece of masking tape. This will help you to hold the silver rectangles in place while you are texturing them, and will also help to keep your fingertips at a safe distance to avoid hitting them with the hammer.

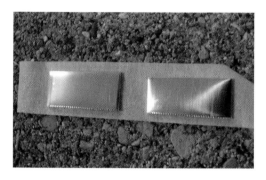

4. Place the piece of masking tape with the silver rectangles sticky side down onto a concrete block or landscape paver.

5. With a hammer, gently strike the tape-covered silver rectangles using a firm strike, but don't hit too hard. You can achieve the desired texture more easily with multiple soft strikes rather than a few hard strikes. Lift the tape frequently and check the progress of the texturing, making sure that the entire surface of the silver rectangles is getting a uniform texture. The surface will look similar to sandpaper if you are using a concrete block. When you achieve the desired texture, remove the silver rectangles from the masking tape.

6. The silver rectangles will have a slight curve to them, and the edges will be misshapen and sharp after you texture them. You can leave the silver rectangles curved or, to flatten them, place the silver rectangles on a hard, flat surface and use a rawhide mallet to flatten them. If you do not have a rawhide mallet, you can place the silver rectangles on a hard, flat surface, cover the pieces with a thick piece of scrap leather, and use a hammer to gently tap the leather covered silver rectangles to flatten them.

7. You will need to use a file to eliminate any rough or sharp edges. Use a fine grit sanding pad to go over the area where you have filed to smooth the edges and remove any file marks.

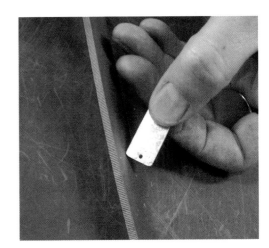

8. Measure ⅟₁₆" from one end of each textured silver rectangle and place a mark in the center of each piece. This is where the holes will be drilled to attach the jump ring and bar components.

9. Put on the safety glasses. Place the textured silver rectangles onto a hard, flat surface. Place the point of the awl on the mark that you made ⅟₁₆" from the end of the rectangle pieces and use a hammer to firmly strike once on the top of the awl to make a pilot hole for drilling the holes into the silver rectangles.

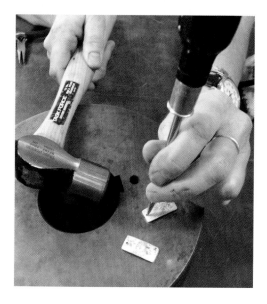

10. Using a ⅟₁₆" drill bit, drill holes into each of the silver rectangles with a handheld rotary tool, flex shaft, or drill press. Remember to wear safety glasses.

11. Use the file or sanding pad to eliminate any burs or rough edges left from drilling holes into the silver rectangles.

12. Apply liver of sulfur or oxidizing solution to the textured silver rectangles, bar components, and jump rings. It is very important to follow any safety recommendations the manufacturer suggests when working with any chemicals.

13. After applying the oxidizing solution, use fine steel wool to remove the darkened areas on the raised surface of the silver rectangles, leaving some of the textured areas dark. Rub the fine steel wool over the jump rings and bar components to remove some but not all of the darkened areas. Rinse with water, dry, and rub with polishing cloth.

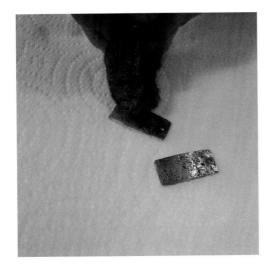

14. With two pair of chain nose pliers pointing up, hold the jump ring with the opening at the top. Roll one of your wrists away from you and your other wrist toward you, opening the jump ring only as much as necessary. To close the jump ring, hold it the same way and roll your wrists in the opposite direction (think of holding a piece of paper and tearing it). Never pull the jump ring ends out as this will weaken the metal, and it will be difficult to close the jump ring.

15. Add the bar component and textured silver rectangle to the jump ring. Close the jump ring.

16. Gently open the loop at the bottom of the ear wire, add the other end of the bar component, and then close the ear wire loop.

17. Repeat these steps for the second earring.

Concrete Textured Sterling Silver Orthoceras Fossil Pendant

MATERIALS NEEDED

One ½" × 1" 18-gauge sterling sheet silver

One ⅞" bar component

Orthoceras fossil with hole at the top

Two 5.3 × 3.2 mm 16-gauge sterling silver oval jump rings

One 6 mm 16-gauge sterling silver round jump ring

Leather cord with clasp

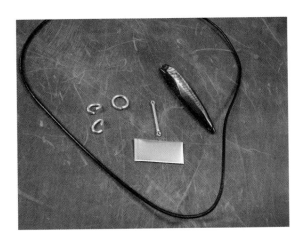

TOOLS NEEDED

Ruler

Marker

Jeweler's saw or tin snips

Masking tape

Concrete block or landscape paver

Hammer

File

Fine grit sanding pad

Awl

1⁄16" drill bit

Handheld rotary tool, flex shaft, or drill press

Liver of sulfur or oxidizing solution

Fine steel wool

Polishing cloth

Two pairs of chain nose pliers

1. Use the ruler to measure and mark one ½" × 1" rectangle piece of 18-gauge sterling sheet silver (if you will be making the earrings and bracelet projects, you may want to cut the rectangle silver pieces needed for the other projects texture them all at one time).

2. Using a jeweler's saw or tin snips, cut the 18-gauge sterling sheet silver into one ½" × 1" rectangle.

3. Place the ½" × 1" sterling silver rectangle onto the sticky side of a piece of masking tape. This will help you hold the silver rectangle in place while you are texturing it; it will also help to keep your fingertips at a safe distance to avoid hitting them with the hammer.

4. Place the piece of masking tape with the silver rectangle sticky side down onto a concrete block or landscape paver.

5. With a hammer, gently strike the tape covered silver rectangle with a firm strike; there is no need to hit it too hard. You can achieve the desired texture more easily with multiple soft strikes rather than a few hard strikes. Lift the tape frequently and check the progress of the texturing, making sure that the entire surface of the silver rectangle is getting a uniform texture. The surface will look similar to sandpaper if you are using a concrete block. When you achieve the desired texture, remove the silver rectangle from the masking tape.

6. The silver rectangle will have a slight curve to it, and the edges will be misshapen and sharp after texturing it. If you like, you can leave the rectangle curved. If you want to flatten it, place the rectangle on a hard, flat surface and use a rawhide mallet to flatten it. If you do not have a rawhide mallet, place the silver rectangle on a hard, flat surface, cover it with a thick piece of scrap leather, and with a hammer gently tap the leather covered silver rectangle to flatten it. You will need to use a file to eliminate any rough or sharp edges. Use a fine grit sanding pad to go over the area where you have filed to smooth the edges and remove any file marks.

7. Measure $\frac{1}{16}$" from each end of the textured silver rectangle and place a mark in the center of the piece; this is where the holes will be drilled to attach the jump ring and bar component and also the jump ring and the Orthocras fossil.

8. Put on the safety glasses. Place the textured silver rectangle onto a hard, flat surface. Place the point of the awl on the mark that you made $\frac{1}{16}$" from each end of the silver rectangle, and firmly strike once on the top of the awl with a hammer to make the pilot holes for drilling the holes into the silver rectangle.

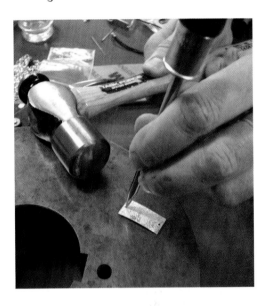

9. Using a $\frac{1}{16}$" drill bit, drill holes into the silver rectangle with a handheld rotary tool, flex shaft, or drill press. Remember to wear safety glasses.

10. Use the file or sanding pad to eliminate any burs or rough edges that remain from drilling holes into the silver rectangle.

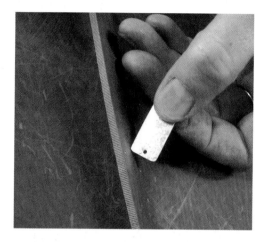

11. Apply liver of sulfur or oxidizing solution to the textured silver rectangle, bar component, and jump rings. It is very important to follow any safety recommendations the manufacturer suggests when working with any chemicals.

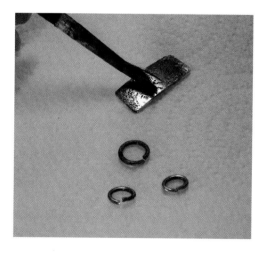

12. After oxidizing the various pieces, use fine steel wool to remove the darkened areas on the raised surface of the silver rectangle, leaving some of the textured areas dark. Rub the fine steel wool over the bar component and jump rings to remove some but not all of the darkened areas. Rinse with water, dry, and rub with polishing cloth.

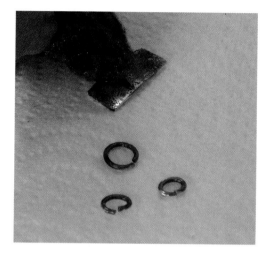

13. With two pair of chain nose pliers pointing up, hold the jump ring with the opening at the top. Roll one of your wrists away from you and your other wrist toward you, opening the jump ring only as much as necessary. (To close the jump ring, hold it the same way and roll your wrists in the opposite direction.) Never pull the jump ring ends out; this will weaken the metal, and it will be difficult to close the jump ring.

14. Using two pairs of chain nose pliers, open the 5.3 × 3.2 mm 16-gauge sterling silver oval jump ring, add the bar component, and then close the jump ring. Open the other oval jump ring and add the textured silver rectangle and the other end of the bar component. Close the jump ring. Open the large 6 mm 16-gauge jump ring and add the Orthoceras fossil and the other end of the textured silver rectangle. Close the jump ring.

15. Slide the oval jump ring at the top of the bar component onto a leather cord or chain.

Concrete Textured Bracelet

MATERIALS NEEDED

Five ½" × 1" sterling sheet silver
Nine 5.3 × 3.2 mm 16-gauge sterling silver oval
   jump rings
One 6 mm 16-gauge sterling silver round jump ring
Sterling silver clasp

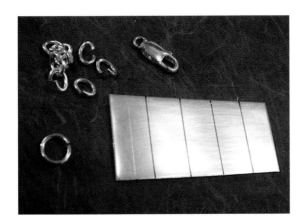

TOOLS NEEDED

Ruler
Marker
Jeweler's saw or tin snips
Masking tape
Concrete block or landscape paver
Hammer
File
Fine grit sanding pad
Awl
$\frac{1}{16}$" drill bit
Handheld rotary tool, flex shaft, or drill press
Liver of sulfur or oxidizing solution
Fine steel wool
Polishing cloth
Two pairs of chain nose pliers

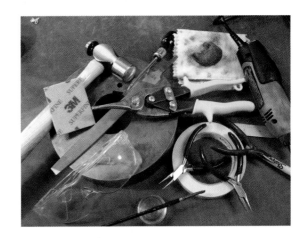

1. Use the ruler to measure and mark five ½" × 1" rectangle pieces of 18-gauge sterling sheet silver.

2. Using a jeweler's saw or tin snips, cut the 18-gauge sterling sheet silver into five ½" × 1" rectangles (if you will be making the earring and pendant projects, you may want to cut all of the rectangle silver pieces needed for the other projects and texture them all at one time).

3. Place the five ½" × 1" sterling silver rectangle pieces onto the sticky side of a piece of masking tape. This will help you to hold the silver rectangles in place while you are texturing them; it will also help to keep your fingertips at a safe distance to avoid hitting them with the hammer.

4. Place the piece of masking tape with the silver rectangles sticky side down onto a concrete block or landscape paver.

5. Gently strike the tape covered silver rectangles with a hammer. When you strike them, use a firm strike; there is no need to hit them very hard. You can achieve the desired texture more easily with multiple soft strikes rather than fewer hard strikes. Lift the tape frequently and check the progress of the texturing, making sure that the entire surface of the silver rectangles is getting a uniform texture. The surface will look similar to sandpaper if you are using a concrete block. When you achieve the desired texture, remove the silver rectangles from the masking tape.

7. Measure ¹⁄₁₆" from each end of the textured silver rectangles and place a mark in the center of each piece; this is where the holes to attach the jump rings will be drilled.

6. The silver rectangles will have a slight curve to them and the edges will be misshapen and sharp after texturing them. You can leave the silver rectangles curved or, to flatten them, place the silver rectangles on a hard, flat surface and use a rawhide mallet to flatten them. If you do not have a rawhide mallet, place the silver rectangles on a hard, flat surface, cover the pieces with a thick piece of scrap leather, and gently tap the leather covered silver rectangles with a hammer to flatten them. You will need to use a file to eliminate any rough or sharp edges. Use a fine grit sanding pad to go over the area where you have filed to smooth the edges and remove any file marks.

8. Put on the safety glasses. Place the textured silver rectangles onto a hard, flat surface. Place the point of the awl on the marks that you made $\frac{1}{16}$" from the end of the rectangle pieces and use a hammer to firmly strike once on the top of the awl to make the pilot holes for drilling the holes into the silver rectangles.

9. Using a $\frac{1}{16}$" drill bit, drill holes into each of the silver rectangles with a handheld rotary tool, flex shaft, or drill press. Remember to wear safety glasses.

10. Use the file or sanding pad to eliminate any burs or rough edges left from drilling holes into the silver rectangles.

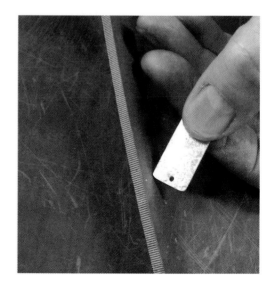

11. Apply liver of sulfur or oxidizing solution to the textured silver rectangles, clasp, and jump rings. It is very important to follow any safety recommendations the manufacturer suggests when working with any chemicals.

12. After oxidizing the various pieces, use fine steel wool to remove the darkened areas on the raised surface of the silver rectangles, leaving some of the textured areas dark. Rub the fine steel wool over the clasp and jump rings to remove some but not all of the darkened areas. Rinse with water, dry, and rub with a polishing cloth.

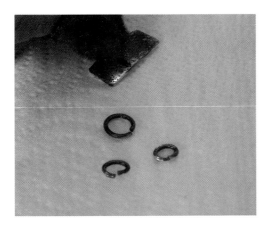

13. With two pair of chain nose pliers pointing up, hold the jump ring with the opening at the top. Roll one of your wrists away from you and your other wrist toward you, opening the jump ring only as much as necessary. (To close the jump ring, hold it the same way and roll your wrists in the opposite direction.) Never pull the jump ring ends out as this will weaken the metal, and it will be difficult to close the jump ring.

14. Using chain nose pliers, open the 5.3 × 3.2 mm 16-gauge sterling silver oval jump ring, add the clasp and one of the textured silver rectangles, and close the jump ring. Alternate as follows: textured silver rectangle, jump ring, textured silver rectangle, jump ring, textured silver rectangle, jump ring, textured silver rectangle, jump ring, textured silver rectangle jump ring, textured silver rectangle.

15. When you have the clasp and five textured silver rectangles all connected with jump rings, add four oval jump rings and one 16-gauge 6 mm round jump ring onto the end of the bracelet.

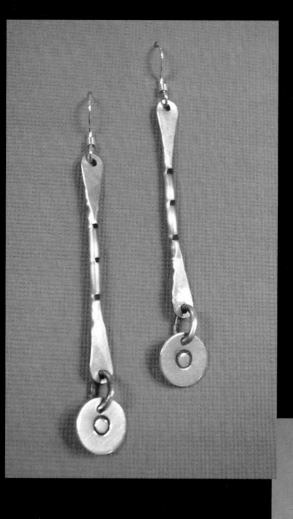
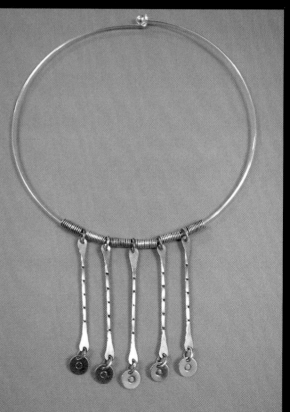

Deco Design Copper and Sterling Silver Earrings and Necklace

Deco Design Copper and Sterling Silver Earrings

These copper and sterling silver beauties will make you feel both trendy and elegant.
And they're so much fun to make!

MATERIALS NEEDED

3" 12-gauge copper wire
Two 5.3 × 3.2 mm sterling silver oval jump rings
Two 3/8" sterling silver discs
Two sterling silver ear wires

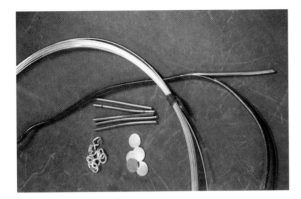

TOOLS NEEDED

Ruler
Marker
Hammer
Wire cutters or tin snips
Hard, flat surface
Flat screwdriver
Nail set punch
Awl
$\frac{1}{16}$" drill bit
Handheld rotary tool, flex shaft, or drill press
File
Fine sanding pad
Two pairs of chain nose pliers
Flat nose pliers
Liver of sulfur or oxidizing solution
Safety glasses
Fine steel wool
Polishing cloth

1. Use the ruler to measure and mark the 12-gauge copper wire. You will need two pieces that are each 1½" long. Use the wire cutters or tin snips to cut the wire.

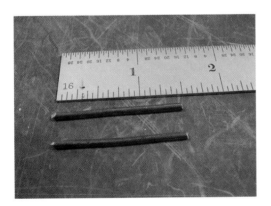

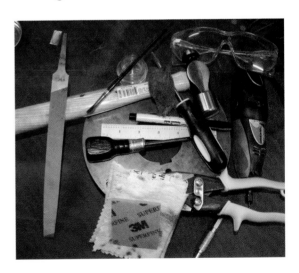

2. Use the ruler to measure and mark both 1½" pieces of 12-gauge copper wire 3/8" from each end of the wire. This will give you a visual guide to use when you flatten the ends of the wire with the hammer.

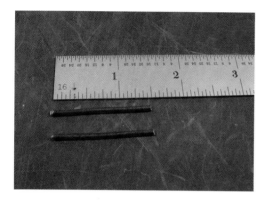

3. Lay the wire pieces onto a hard, flat surface and use a hammer to strike the end of the wire with a firm tap, using the 3/8" mark that you made on the end of the copper wire as a visual guide on where to strike the wire. You may need to strike the copper wire multiple times to achieve the flatness necessary to allow sufficient space to drill the holes. Do this step to both ends of the copper wire.

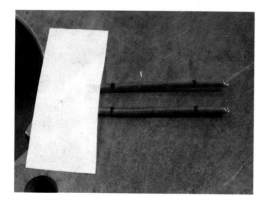

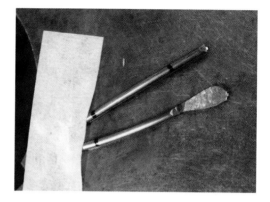

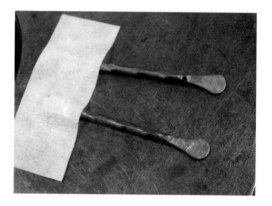

4. The ends of the copper wire will be sharp after hammering them flat, so use a file to eliminate any sharp or rough edges. After filing the edges, use a fine grit sanding pad to go over the area where you have filed to smooth the edges and eliminate any file marks. Do this to both ends of the copper wire pieces.

5. Use the ruler to measure and mark the center of each 1½" piece of copper wire. Use the ruler to measure and mark ¼" increments up and down both of the 1½" copper wires. This will be where you stamp the copper wires.

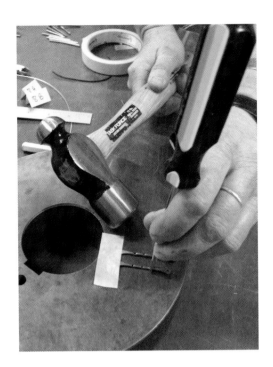

6. After marking the wires, place them onto a hard, flat surface. You can use a piece of masking tape on the ends of the wires to hold them in place. Place the end of the flat screwdriver onto the mark that you made on the copper wire and firmly strike the top of the screwdriver once with a hammer. You do not want to strike the screwdriver too hard as it will make the wire too thin and brittle. Do this to all of the marks that you made on the two copper wire pieces. If needed, use the fine grit sanding pad or steel wool to remove any marker lines left on the copper wire. Set these aside.

7. Place the round discs onto a hard, flat surface. You can use masking tape on the edges of the discs to keep them in place while you stamp them. Select a nail set punch. (These are inexpensive and can be purchased at any home improvement store. They usually come in sets of three sizes; mix up the sizes or choose just one size to stamp your circles.)

8. Place the nail set punch on the top of the disc and use the hammer to firmly strike the top of the nail set punch, creating a stamped circle shape on the disc. If desired, you can mark the discs where you want to stamp them before you begin. When you strike the top of the nail set punch, strike it only once. If you strike the top of the nail set punch multiple times, the punch may skip across the silver and scratch the surface of the disc.

9. Use the ruler to measure and mark $\frac{1}{16}$" from the edge of the discs. This is where the holes will be drilled to attach the discs to the copper wire pieces.

10. Use the ruler to measure and mark $\frac{1}{16}$" from the end of the copper wire where you have flattened the wire. This is where you will drill the holes to attach the discs and the ear wires.

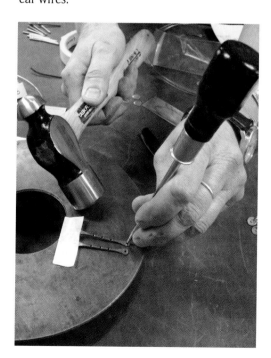

11. Put on the safety glasses. Place the copper wire and the discs onto a hard, flat surface. Place the point of the awl on the marks that you made $\frac{1}{16}$" from the end of the wire and the edge of the discs. Using a hammer, firmly strike the top of the awl once to make a pilot hole for drilling the holes into each end of the copper wire and each of the discs.

12. Using a $\frac{1}{16}$" drill bit, drill holes into each end of the pieces of copper wire and each of the discs using a handheld rotary tool, flex shaft, or drill press. (Of course, wearing your safety glasses.)

13. Use the file or sanding pad to eliminate any burs or rough edges left from drilling holes into the pieces of copper wire and the discs.

14. Apply liver of sulfur or oxidizing solution to the discs and the two pieces of copper wire. It is very important to follow any safety recommendations the manufacturer suggests when using any chemicals.

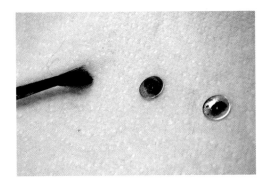

15. After using the oxidizing solution, use fine steel wool to remove some of the darkened area on the surface of the discs and the two pieces of copper wire, leaving the circles and the lines where you stamped dark. Rinse with water, dry, and rub with a polishing cloth.

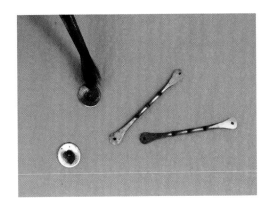

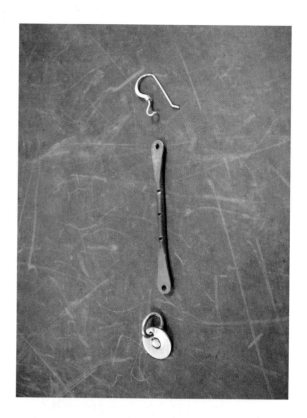

16. With two pairs of chain nose pliers pointing up, hold the jump ring with the opening at the top. Roll one of your wrists away from you and your other wrist toward you, opening the jump ring only as much as necessary. To close the jump ring, hold it the same way and roll your wrists in the opposite direction. Never pull the jump ring ends out; this will weaken the metal, and it will be difficult to close the jump ring.

17. Using two pairs of chain nose pliers, open a jump ring and attach the disc to one end of the copper wire. Repeat this with the other disc and copper wire.

18. Use chain nose pliers to gently open the loop at the bottom of the ear wire and add the other end of the copper wire. Close the ear wire loop. Repeat with the second earring.

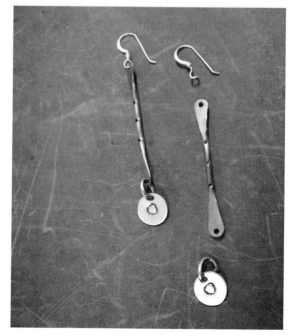

Deco Design Copper and Sterling Silver Necklace

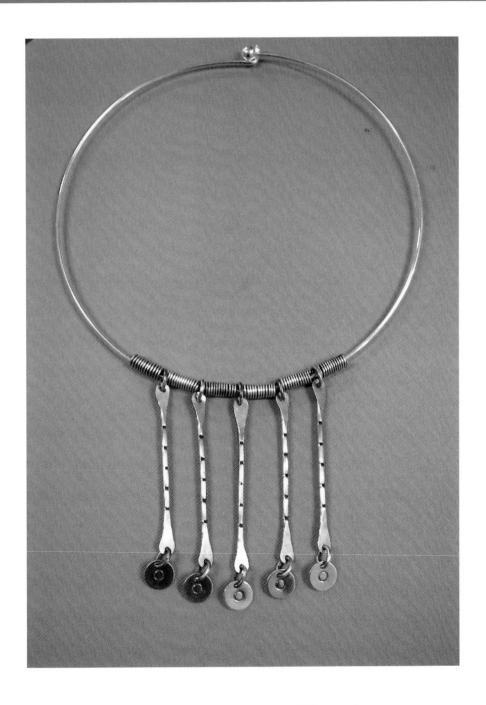

MATERIALS NEEDED

10" 12-gauge copper wire
Ten 5.3 × 3.2 mm sterling silver oval jump rings
Five 3/8" sterling silver discs
36" 20-gauge sterling silver wire (for coil beads)
Neck wire

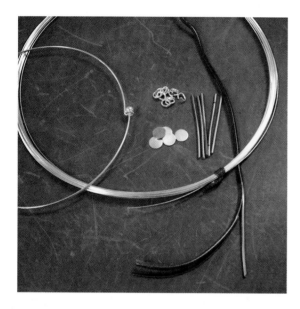

TOOLS NEEDED

Ruler
Marker
Hammer
Wire cutters or tin snips
Hard, flat surface
Flat screwdriver
Nail set punch
Awl
1/16" drill bit
Handheld rotary tool, flex shaft, or drill press
File
Fine sanding pad
Bamboo skewer
Two pairs of chain nose pliers
Flat nose pliers
Liver of sulfur or oxidizing solution
Safety glasses
Fine steel wool
Polishing cloth

1. Use the ruler to measure and mark the 12-gauge copper wire. You will need five pieces that are each 2" long. Use the wire cutters or tin snips to cut the wire.

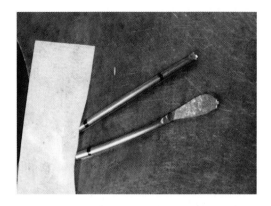

2. Use the ruler to measure and mark the 2" pieces of 12-gauge copper wire 3/8" from each end of the wire. This will give you a visual guide to use when you flatten the ends of the wire with the hammer.

3. Lay the wire pieces onto a hard, flat surface and use a hammer to strike the end of the wire with a firm tap using the 3/8" mark that you made on the end of the copper wire as a visual guide. You may need to strike the copper wire multiple times to achieve the flatness necessary to allow sufficient space to drill the holes. Do this step to both ends of the copper wire.

4. The ends of the copper wire will be sharp after hammering them flat. Use a file to eliminate any sharp or rough edges. After filing the edges, use a fine grit sanding pad to go over the area where you have filed to smooth the edges and eliminate any file marks. Do this to both ends of the copper wire pieces.

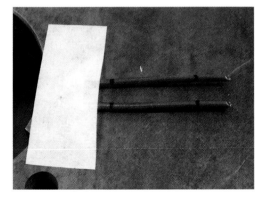

5. Use the ruler to measure and mark the center of each 2" piece of copper wire. Use the ruler to measure and mark ¼" increments up and down all of the 2" copper wires. This will be where you stamp the copper wires.

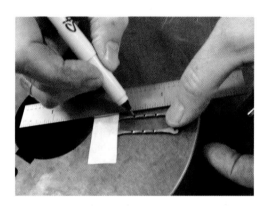

6. After marking the wires, place them onto a hard, flat surface. You can use a piece of masking tape on the ends of the wires to hold them in place. Place the end of the flat screwdriver onto the marks that you made on the copper wires and firmly strike the top of the screwdriver once with the hammer. You do not want to strike the screwdriver too hard; this will make the wire too thin and brittle. Do this to all of the marks that you made on all five copper wire pieces. If the copper wire pieces become curved, just turn them over on the hard, flat surface and gently tap them with a hammer to straighten them. Set these aside.

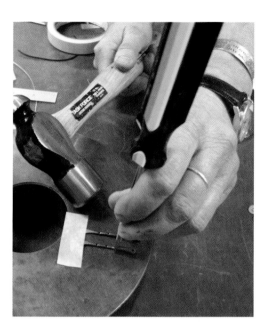

7. Place the round discs onto a hard flat surface. You can use masking tape on the edges of the discs to keep them in place while you stamp them. Select a nail set punch. (These are inexpensive and can be purchased at any home improvement store. They usually come in sets of three sizes; mix up the sizes or choose just one size to stamp your circles.)

8. Place the nail set punch on the top of the disc and firmly strike the top of the nail set punch with the hammer to create a stamped circle shape on the disc. If desired, you can mark the discs where you want to stamp them before you begin. When you strike the top of the nail set punch, strike it only once. If you strike the top of the nail set punch multiple times, the punch may skip across the silver and scratch the surface of the discs.

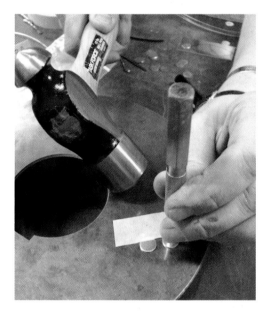

9. Use the ruler to measure and mark $\frac{1}{16}$" from the edge of the discs. This is where the holes will be drilled to attach the discs to the copper wire pieces.

10. Use the ruler to measure and mark $\frac{1}{16}$" from the end of the copper wire where you have flattened the wire. This is where you will drill the holes to attach the discs and the jump rings.

11. Put on the safety glasses. Place the copper wire and the discs onto a hard, flat surface. Place the point of the awl on the marks that you made $\frac{1}{16}$" from the end of the wire and the edge of the discs. Using a hammer, firmly strike the top of the awl once to make a pilot hole for drilling the holes into each end of the 12-gauge wire and each of the discs.

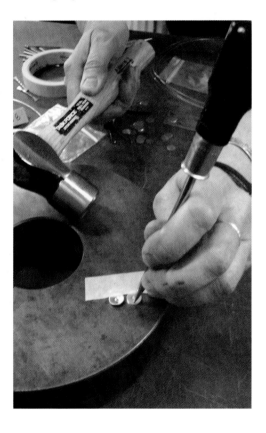

12. Using a $\frac{1}{16}$" drill bit, drill holes into each end of the pieces of copper wire and each of the discs using a handheld rotary tool, flex shaft, or drill press. (Of course, wearing your safety glasses.)

13. Use the file or sanding pad to eliminate any burs or rough edges left from drilling holes into the pieces of copper wire and the discs. Set these aside.

14. Use the ruler to measure and mark the 20-gauge wire into six 6" pieces. Using your hands, wrap each piece of the 6" wire around the bamboo skewer to form the coil beads. Use the chain nose or flat nose pliers to help finish the last coil. If needed, trim and file the ends of the wire.

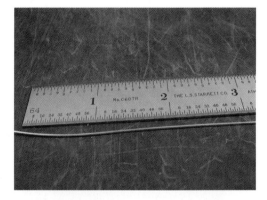

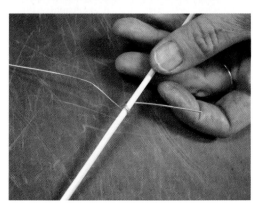

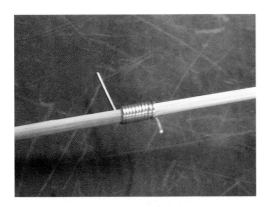

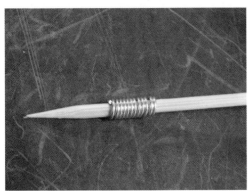

15. Apply liver of sulfur or oxidizing solution to the discs, two pieces of copper wire, and the coil beads. It is very important to follow any safety recommendations the manufacturer suggests when using any chemicals.

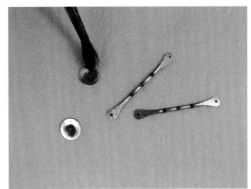

16. After oxidizing the various pieces, use fine steel wool to remove some of the darkened area on the surface of the discs, the two pieces of copper wire, and the coil beads, leaving the circles and the lines where you stamped dark. Rinse with water, dry, and rub with a polishing cloth.

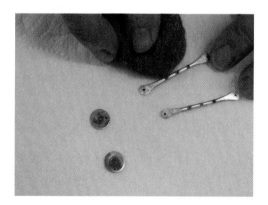

17. With two pair of chain nose pliers pointing up, hold the jump ring with the opening at the top. Roll one of your wrists away from you and your other wrist toward you, opening the jump ring only as much as necessary. To close the jump ring, hold it the same way and roll your wrists in the opposite direction. Never pull the jump ring ends out; this will weaken the metal, and it will be difficult to close the jump ring.

18. Using two pairs of chain nose pliers, open a jump ring and attach the disc to one end of the copper wire. Repeat this with the other discs and pieces of copper wire. Add a jump ring to the other end of each of the copper wires.

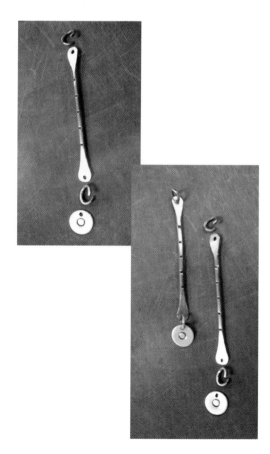

19. Place the components onto the neck wire in the following order: Wire coil bead, jump ring with copper wire and disc, wire coil bead, jump ring with copper wire and disc, wire coil bead, jump ring with copper wire and disc wire coil bead, jump ring with copper wire and disc, wire coil bead, jump ring with copper wire and disc, wire coil bead.

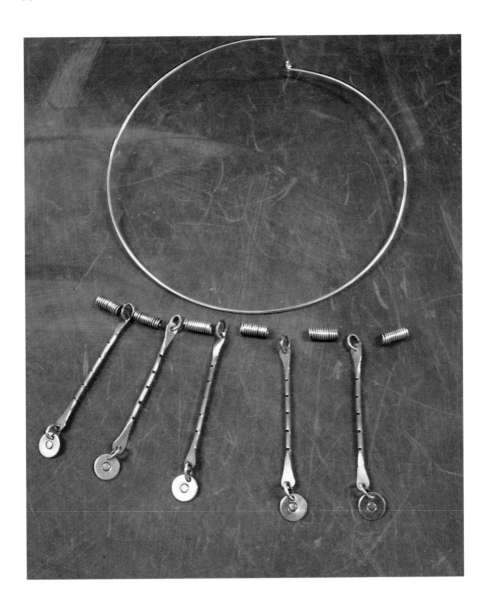

Sterling Silver Stamped Nature Earrings and Necklace

Sterling Silver Stamped Leaf and Seed Bead Earrings

Change the bead colors on the gorgeous sterling silver leaf background to coordinate with the seasons or your outfit.

MATERIALS NEEDED

Two ½" × 1" pieces of 18-gauge sterling sheet silver

Two 1½" eye pins

Two ½" pieces of 1.7 mm black hollow rubber tube

Two 1½" head pins

24 seed beads

Two 16-gauge 5.3 × 3.2 mm sterling silver
       oval jump rings

Two sterling silver ear wires

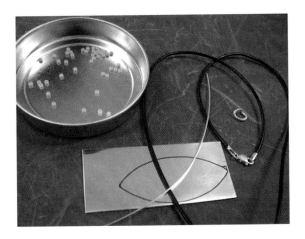

TOOLS NEEDED

Ruler

Marker

Jeweler's saw or tin snips

Hard, flat surface

Rawhide mallet

Fine grit sanding pad

Safety glasses

Awl

Hammer

$\frac{1}{16}$" drill bit

Handheld rotary tool, flex shaft, or drill press

Masking tape

Flat screwdriver

Liver of sulfur or oxidizing solution

Fine steel wool

Polishing cloth

Scissors

Round nose pliers

Two pairs of chain nose pliers

1. Decide on the shape of the leaves that you want to use and draw the shape with a marker onto two ½" × 1" pieces of 18-gauge sterling sheet silver. You can free-hand draw the leaf shape or use a design from a wide selection of available clip art. You can make the leaves exactly the same, or you might make them different from each other for added interest. You may find that using a simple shape will be easier when you do this project the first time.

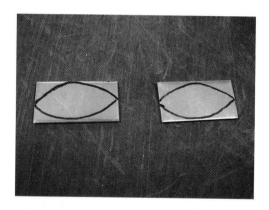

3. The edges of the leaf shapes will be sharp after you cut them out, so you will need to use a file to refine the shape of the leaves and to eliminate any sharp corners or rough edges. After filing, use a fine grit sanding pad to go over the area where you have filed to smooth the edges and remove any file marks. Do this step to both leaf shapes.

2. Using a jeweler's saw or tin snips, cut the leaf shapes from the ½" × 1" 18-gauge sterling sheet silver. If you are using tin snips and not a jeweler's saw, cut outside of the marker line you drew. This will allow you room to refine the edges with the file after the leaf shapes are cut out. In addition, if you use tin snips to cut out the pieces; they will not be flat after you cut them. You will need to place the leaf shapes on a hard, flat surface and use a rawhide mallet to flatten them. If you do not have a rawhide mallet, place the leaf shapes on a hard, flat surface, cover the pieces with a thick piece of scrap leather, and gently tap the leather covered leaf shapes with a hammer to flatten them.

4. Measure ¹⁄₁₆" from each tip of the leaf shapes and place a mark. This is where the holes to attach the oval jump ring and eye pin with the black hollow rubber tube will be drilled.

5. Put on your safety glasses. Place the sterling silver leaf shapes onto a hard, flat surface. Put the point of the awl on the mark that you made ¹⁄₁₆" from the point of the leaf shape and use a hammer to firmly strike the top of the awl once to make a pilot hole for drilling holes into the leaf shapes.

6. Using a ¹⁄₁₆" drill bit, drill holes into each of the leaf shapes using a handheld rotary tool, flex shaft, or drill press (don't forget your safety glasses).

7. Use the file or sanding pad to eliminate any burs or rough edges left from drilling the holes into the leaf shapes.

8. Use the fine grit sanding pad to go over the surface of the leaf shapes to give them some organic texture and to achieve a brushed finish on the surface. You could also use a steel brush, or green kitchen scrubber, and use the hammering technique described in Chapter 9, or the concrete textured technique from Chapter 6 for the surface finish on the leaf shapes.

9. Decide where you would like the leaf "vein" placement to be. You can use a marker to draw where you would like them to be or just randomly place them on the leaf shapes.

10. Put your safety glasses on. Place the leaf shapes onto a hard, flat surface. I use masking tape on the tip to hold the leaf shapes in place while I am stamping the veins into them. Place the tip of the flat screwdriver onto the leaf shape and strike the top of the flat screwdriver once. If you strike the top of the screwdriver multiple times, it is likely to jump across the surface of the leaf shapes and leave marks on the surface that you had not intended. Oops! If that happens, consider it a learning experience and adjust your original design.

11. Apply liver of sulfur or an oxidizing solution to the leaf shapes and oval jump rings. It is very important to follow any safety recommendations that the manufacturer suggests when using any chemicals.

12. After oxidizing the various pieces, use fine steel wool to remove the darkened area on the raised surface of the leaf shapes, leaving the "veins" dark. Rub the fine steel wool over the jump rings to remove some but not all of the darkened areas. Rinse with water, dry, and rub with polishing cloth. Set these aside.

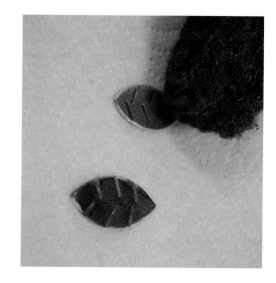

13. Use the ruler to measure and mark the rubber tube into two pieces measuring ½" each. Cut the rubber tube with scissors. Slide the ½" pieces of rubber tube onto the 1½" eye pins with the existing loop at the bottom.

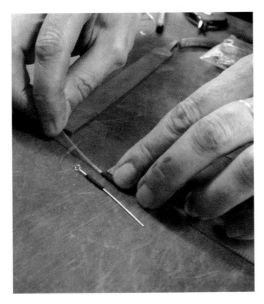

14. Use the ruler to measure and mark 5⁄16" above the top of the rubber tube on the eye pin. Cut the eye pin wire 5⁄16" above the top of the black hollow tube.

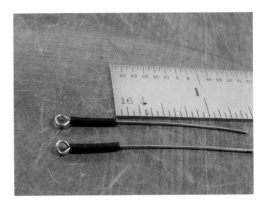

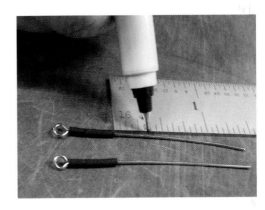

15. Use the chain nose pliers to bend the eye pin wire next to the top of the black hollow tube at a 90-degree angle.

16. Hold the eye pin wire with the rubber tube on it in one hand with the wire that you bent pointing toward you. Using the round nose pliers, grip the end of the eye pin wire that is pointing toward you and roll it away from you. Your hand position will be similar to that of holding a bicycle handlebar. At this point, the loop at the top of the eye pin wire should be large enough to slip the ear wire on. After you add the ear wire, use the round nose pliers to grasp the loop of the eye pin wire and roll it closed. You can use the round nose or chain nose pliers to adjust the shape of the loop at the top of the eye pin if you need to.

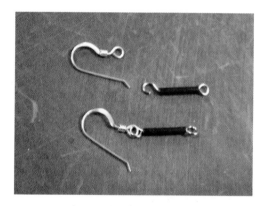

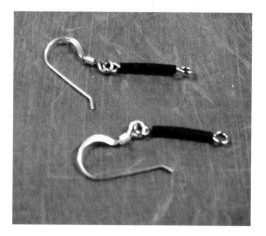

17. Repeat these steps for the second eye pin. Set these aside.

It will become easier to keep the loop round in shape the more that you do this technique. An alternative to using a ruler to measure the spot to cut off the eye pin at $5/16$" above the black hollow tube is to designate a bead that is $5/16$" long or a piece of hollow tube cut to $5/16$" and slide it onto the top of the eye pin and cut the wire directly above it. This will allow you to have uniform length on all of these that you do.

I use base metal head pins and eye pins for strength on projects that use a loop closure at the top. Base metal is stronger than sterling silver, and you will not need to worry about the loop coming open. I do use sterling silver for the ear wires; some people are sensitive to base metal because of the nickel content when it comes in direct contact with their skin.

18. Slide 12 seed beads onto the head pin. Use the same technique that was used on the eye pins to form a loop at the top of the head pin in Steps 14 through 17.

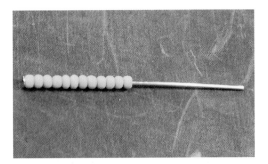

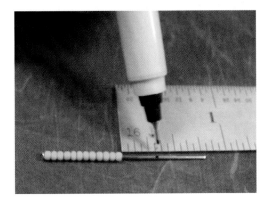

To open and close jump rings, use two pairs of chain nose pliers pointing up to hold the jump ring with the opening at the top. Roll one of your wrists away from you and your other wrist toward you, opening the jump ring only as much as necessary. To close the jump ring, hold it the same way and roll your wrists in the opposite directions. (Think of holding a piece of paper and tearing it.) Never pull the jump ring ends out; this will weaken the metal, and it will be difficult to close the jump ring.

19. Using two pair of chain nose pliers, open the oval jump ring and slide the bottom of the eye pin with the rubber tube, top loop of the head pin with the seed beads, and the sterling silver leaf shape onto the jump ring. Close the jump ring and repeat this step for the other earring.

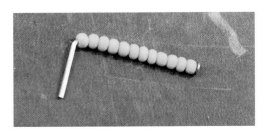

Sterling Silver Stamped Leaf and Seed Bead Necklace

MATERIALS NEEDED

¾" × 2" piece of 18-gauge sterling sheet silver
Approximately 4" 20-gauge sterling silver wire
Seed beads (approximately 25)
One 16-gauge 5.3 × 3.2 mm sterling silver
        oval jump ring
Leather cord with clasp

TOOLS NEEDED

Ruler
Marker
Jeweler's saw or tin snips
Hard, flat surface
Rawhide mallet
File
Fine grit sanding pad
Safety glasses
Awl or punch
Hammer
¹⁄₁₆" drill bit
Handheld rotary tool, flex shaft, or drill press
Masking tape
Flat screwdriver
Liver of sulfur or oxidizing solution
Fine steel wool
Polishing cloth
Scissors
Round nose pliers
Two pairs of chain nose pliers

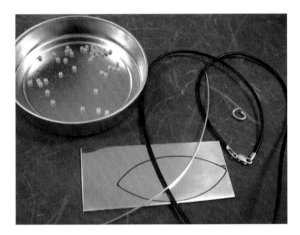

1. Decide on the shape of the leaf that you want to use and draw the shape with a marker onto the ¾" × 2" piece of 18-gauge sterling sheet silver. You can free-hand draw the leaf shape or use a design from a wide selection of available clip art. If you are making the necklace and earring projects, you can match the necklace leaf shape to the shape of the earring leaves or make them different from each other for added interest. You may find that using a simple shape will be easier the first time you do this project.

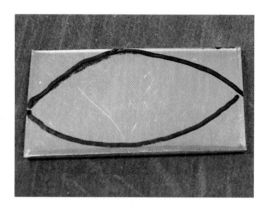

2. Use a jeweler's saw or tin snips to cut the leaf shape from the ¾" × 2" 18-gauge sterling sheet silver. If you are using tin snips and not a jeweler's saw, cut outside of the marker line you drew. This will allow you room to refine the edges with the file after the leaf shape is cut out. When you use tin snips to cut out the leaf shape, it will not be flat after you cut it. You will need to place the leaf shape on a hard, flat surface and use a rawhide mallet to flatten it. If you do not have a rawhide mallet, you can place the leaf shape on a hard, flat surface, cover the piece with a thick piece of scrap leather, and gently tap the leather covered leaf shape with a hammer to flatten it.

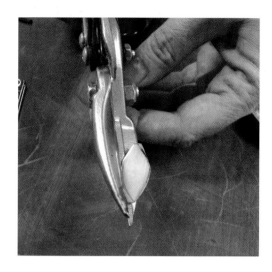

3. The edges of the leaf shape will be sharp after you cut them out, so you will need to use a file to refine the shape of the leaf and to eliminate any sharp corners or rough edges. After filing the edges of the leaf shape, use a fine grit sanding pad to go over the area where you have filed to smooth the edges and remove any file marks.

4. Measure $\frac{1}{16}$" from the top tip of the leaf shape and place a mark where you will be drilling a hole. This will be where you will attach it to the jump ring and onto the leather cord.

5. Put on your safety glasses. Place the sterling silver leaf shape onto a hard, flat surface. Place the point of the awl on the mark that you made $\frac{1}{16}$" from the top point of the leaf shape and use a hammer to firmly strike the top of the awl once to make a pilot hole for drilling the hole into the leaf shape.

6. Using a $\frac{1}{16}$" drill bit, drill a hole into the leaf shape using a handheld rotary tool, flex shaft, or drill press (don't forget your safety glasses).

7. Use the file or sanding pad to eliminate any burs or rough edges left from drilling the hole into the leaf shape.

8. After you drill the hole for attaching the leaf shape to the leather cord, you will measure and mark on the leaf shape where you will be drilling holes to run the wire with the seed beads on it through the leaf shape. Measure $\frac{1}{16}$" down from the hole that you just drilled for the jump ring and place a mark on the leaf shape. Measure $\frac{1}{16}$" from the bottom point of the leaf shape and mark that spot.

9. Put on your safety glasses. Place the leaf shape onto a hard, flat surface. Place the point of the awl on the marks that you made $\frac{1}{16}$" from the top hole and the mark that you made $\frac{1}{16}$" from the bottom point of the leaf shape. Use a hammer to firmly strike the top of the awl once to make a pilot hole for drilling holes into the leaf shape.

10. Using a $\frac{1}{16}$" drill bit, drill holes into the leaf shape using a handheld rotary tool, flex shaft, or drill press (of course, you're wearing your safety glasses).

11. Use the file or sanding pad to eliminate any burs or rough edges left from drilling holes into the leaf shape.

12. Use the fine grit sanding pad to go over the surface of the leaf shape to give it some organic texture and to achieve a brushed finish on the surface. You could also use a steel brush, green kitchen scrubber, the hammering technique from project #8, or the concrete textured technique from Chapter 6 for the surface finish on the leaf shape.

13. Decide where you would like the leaf "vein" placement to be. You can use a marker to draw where you would like them or just randomly place them on the leaf shape.

14. Put on your safety glasses! Place the leaf shape onto a hard, flat surface. I use masking tape on the tip to hold the leaf shape in place while I am stamping the veins into it. Place the tip of the flat screwdriver onto the leaf shape and strike the top of the flat screwdriver once. If you strike the top of the screwdriver multiple times, it is likely to jump across the surface of the leaf shape and leave marks on the surface that you had not intended. If that happens, consider it a learning experience and adjust your original design.

15. Apply liver of sulfur or an oxidizing solution to the leaf shape and oval jump rings. It is very important to follow any safety recommendations that the manufacturer suggests when using any chemicals.

16. After using the oxidizing solution, use fine steel wool to remove the darkened area on the raised surface of the leaf shape, leaving the "veins" dark. Rub the fine steel wool over the jump rings to remove some but not all of the darkened areas. Rinse with water, dry, and rub with polishing cloth. Set these aside.

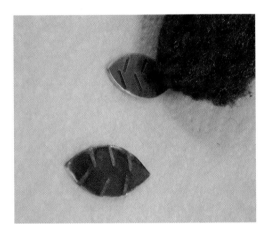

17. Measure the distance from the two holes drilled for the wire and seed beads and add 1½" to that length. This will allow extra wire so that you can secure the wire to the leaf shape. After you cut the wire to the desired length, measure and mark ¾" from one end of the 20-gauge wire.

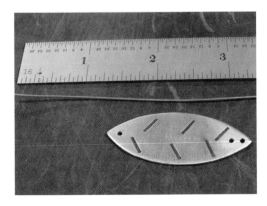

18. Using round nose pliers, curl one end of the 20-gauge wire into a spiral, stopping at the ¾" mark that you made on the wire. With chain nose pliers, bend the wire so that you have a 90-degree angle next to the spiral. This wire will go through the hole in the leaf shape, and you will place the seed beads on it.

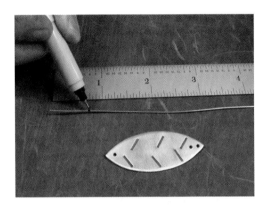

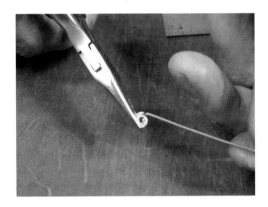

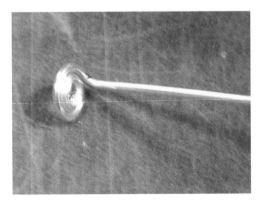

19. Pull the wire through the leaf shape with the spiral on the back. On the front of the leaf shape, add seed beads to the wire. When you have added enough beads on the wire to fill the distance between the two holes in the leaf shape, bend the wire down at a 90-degree angle and thread it through the hole at the bottom point of the leaf shape. When the wire is through the back of the leaf shape, use the round nose pliers and curl the end of the wire into a spiral. Make sure the wire with the seed beads is tight across the front. Bend the spiral flat against the back of the leaf shape to hold the wire and seed beads firmly in place.

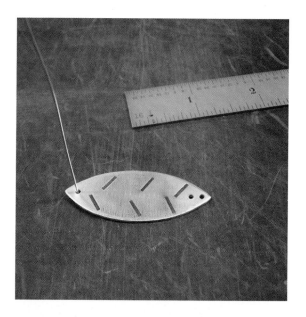

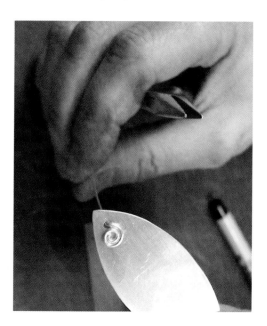

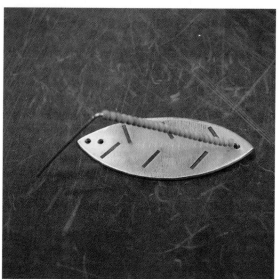

20. Using two pairs of chain nose pliers, open the jump ring and slide it through the hole that is at the top of the leaf shape, close the jump ring, and add it to a leather cord.

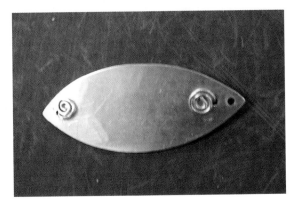

Sea Treasures Hammered Sterling Silver Earrings, Bracelet, and Necklace

Hammered Sterling Silver Fish and Chain Earrings

These little fish earrings are fun to make and even more fun to wear.

MATERIALS NEEDED

½" × 2½" 18-gauge sterling sheet silver
Two 5.3 × 3.2 mm sterling silver oval jump rings
Two ¾" sterling silver chains (1½" total)
Two sterling silver ear wires

TOOLS NEEDED

Hard, flat surface
Ball peen hammer
Marker
Jeweler's saw or tin snips
Rawhide mallet or piece of thick scrap leather
Flat hammer
File
Fine grit sanding pad
Ruler
Safety glasses
Awl
¹⁄₁₆" drill bit
Handheld rotary tool, flex shaft, or drill press
Liver of sulfur or oxidizing solution
Fine steel wool
Polishing cloth
Two pairs of chain nose pliers

What advice would you offer a beginning artist?

"Make sure you have some business sense or have someone with a good business head to represent you."

—Susie Beiman,
Retail Gift Gallery Owner/Buyer

1. Place the ½" × 2½" piece of 18-gauge sterling sheet silver onto a hard, flat surface. (For this project, I used a regular ball peen hammer purchased at a home improvement store. There are many great jeweler's hammers available, but if you are just starting out making jewelry, you may want to start with this inexpensive version.) Use the round end of the ball peen hammer to strike the surface of the sheet silver multiple times, making a uniform hammered texture. If you will be making the bracelet and necklace projects, you may want to texture all of the sterling sheet silver pieces at the same time.

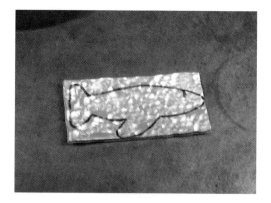

2. Decide on the shapes of the fish that you want to use and draw the shapes with a marker onto the ½" × 2½" piece of 18-gauge sterling sheet silver. You can free-hand draw the fish shapes, or you can use a design from a wide selection of available clip art. You can make the fish shapes identical or make them different from each other for added interest. You may find that using a simple shape will be easier the first time you do this project.

3. Using a jeweler's saw or tin snips, cut the fish shapes from the ½" × 2½" 18-gauge hammered sterling sheet silver. If you are using tin snips and not a jeweler's saw, you will want to cut outside the marker line you drew around the fish shapes. This will allow you room to refine the edges with the file after the fish shapes are cut out. In addition, if you used tin snips, the pieces will not be flat after you cut them. Place the fish shapes on a hard, flat surface and use a rawhide mallet to flatten them. If you do not have a rawhide mallet, you can place the fish shapes on a hard, flat surface, cover the pieces with a thick piece of scrap leather, and gently tap the leather covered fish shapes with a flat hammer to flatten them.

4. The edges of the fish shapes will be sharp after you cut them out, so use a file to refine the shape of the fish and to eliminate any sharp corners or rough edges. After you file the edges, use a fine grit sanding pad to go over the area where you filed to smooth the edges and remove any file marks. Do this step to each fish shape.

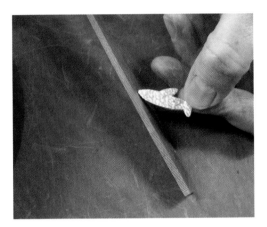

5. Measure $\frac{1}{16}$" from one tip of the fish shapes and place a mark where you want to drill the holes (this is where you will attach them to the oval jump rings and the $\frac{1}{2}$" silver chain). You can place the holes on the same end of the fish shapes, or you can place the holes so that one fish is swimming upstream and one is swimming downstream!

6. Put on the safety glasses. Place the fish shapes onto a hard, flat surface and put the point of the awl on the mark that you made $\frac{1}{16}$" from the edge of the fish shape. Using a hammer, firmly strike the top of the awl once to make a pilot hole for drilling holes into the fish shapes.

7. Using a $\frac{1}{16}$" drill bit, drill holes into each of the fish shapes using a handheld rotary tool, flex shaft, or drill press (don't forget to wear your safety glasses).

8. Use the file or sanding pad to eliminate any burs or rough edges left from drilling the holes into the fish shapes.

9. Use the ruler to measure the chain into 3/4" pieces. Use the wire cutters to cut the chain and then set these pieces aside.

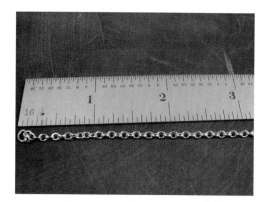

10. Apply liver of sulfur or an oxidizing solution to the fish shapes, chain, and oval jump rings. It is very important to follow any safety recommendations the manufacturer suggests when using any chemicals.

11. After oxidizing the various pieces, use fine steel wool to remove some but not all of the oxidizing solution from the surface of the fish shapes, jump rings, and chain. Rinse with water, dry, and rub with polishing cloth.

To open and close jump rings, use two pair of chain nose pliers pointing up to hold the jump ring with the opening at the top. Roll one of your wrists away from you and your other wrist toward you, opening the jump ring only as much as you need to. To close the jump ring, hold it the same way and roll your wrists in the opposite direction (think of holding a piece of paper and tearing it). Never pull the jump ring ends out, as this will weaken the metal, and it will be difficult to close the jump ring.

13. Use pliers to gently open the loop at the bottom of the ear wire and slide the end link of the chain that is at the opposite end of the fish shape and jump ring onto the loop. Close the loop at the bottom of the ear wire. Repeat this step on the other earring.

12. Open the oval jump ring and add one fish shape and the end link of a ½" piece of chain. Close the jump ring. Repeat with the other jump ring, fish shape, and chain.

Hammered Sterling
Silver Fish and Chain Bracelet

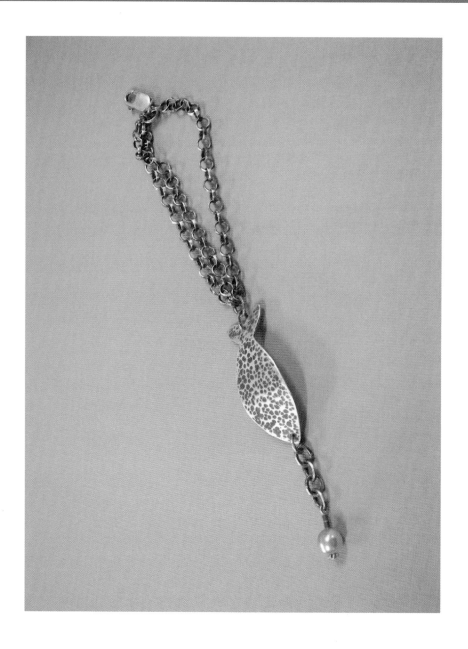

MATERIALS NEEDED

2" × ¾" 18-gauge sterling sheet silver
Eight 5.3 × 3.2 mm sterling silver oval jump rings
One 1½" head pin
One pearl bead
Three small sterling silver beads
Three 3¾" pieces of sterling silver chain
One sterling silver 16 mm lobster clasp

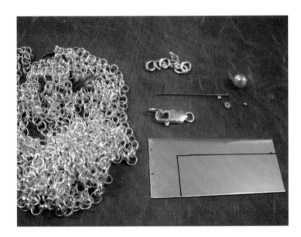

TOOLS NEEDED

Hard, flat surface
Ball peen hammer
Marker
Jeweler's saw or tin snips
Rawhide mallet or piece of thick scrap leather
Flat hammer
File
Ruler
Fine grit sanding pad
Safety glasses
Awl
1/16" drill bit
Handheld rotary tool, flex shaft, or drill press
Two pairs of chain nose pliers
Wire cutters or tin snips
Round nose pliers
Liver of sulfur or oxidizing solution
Fine steel wool
Polishing cloth

1. Place the 2 × ¾" piece of 18-gauge sterling sheet silver onto a hard, flat surface. (For this project I used a regular ball peen hammer purchased at a home improvement store. There are many great jeweler's hammers available, but if you are just starting out making jewelry, you may want to start with this inexpensive version.) Use the round end of the ball peen hammer to strike the surface of the sheet silver multiple times, making a uniform hammered texture. If you will also make the earring and necklace projects, you may want to texture all of the sterling sheet silver pieces at the same time.

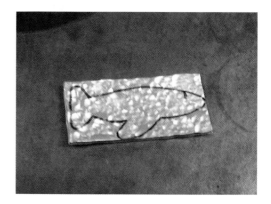

2. Decide on the shape of the fish that you want to use and draw the shape with marker onto the 2 × ¾" piece of the sterling sheet silver. You can free-hand draw the fish shape or you can use a design from a wide selection of available clip art. You may find that using a simple shape will be easier the first time you do this project.

3. Using a jeweler's saw or tin snips, cut the fish shape from the 2" × 2¾" hammered sterling sheet silver. If you are using tin snips and not a jeweler's saw, cut outside the marker line drawn around the fish shape to allow you room to refine the edges with the file after the fish shape is cut out. If you used tin snips, the piece will not be flat after you cut it, so you will need to place the fish shape on a hard, flat surface and use a rawhide mallet to flatten it. If you do not have a rawhide mallet, place the fish shape on a hard, flat surface, cover the piece with a thick piece of scrap leather, and gently tap the leather covered fish shape with a flat hammer to flatten it.

6. Put on the safety glasses. Place the fish shape onto a hard, flat surface and put the point of the awl on the marks that you made $\frac{1}{16}$" from the edge of the fish shape. Use a hammer to firmly strike the top of the awl once to make pilot holes for drilling holes into the fish shape.

4. The edges of the fish shape will be sharp after you cut it out. Use a file to refine the shape of the fish and to eliminate any sharp corners or rough edges. After filing use a fine grit sanding pad to go over the area where you filed to smooth the edges and remove any file marks.

5. Measure $\frac{1}{16}$" from each tip of the fish shape and place a mark where you will be drilling the holes to attach the clasp and the three $3\frac{3}{4}$" pieces of silver chain.

7. Using a $\frac{1}{16}$" drill bit, drill holes into the fish shape using a handheld rotary tool, flex shaft, or drill press (don't forget to wear your safety glasses).

8. Use the file or sanding pad to eliminate any burs or rough edges left from drilling the holes into the fish shape.

9. Apply liver of sulfur or an oxidizing solution to the fish shape, chain, clasp, and jump rings. It is very important to follow any safety recommendations the manufacturer suggests when using any chemicals.

10. After oxidizing the various pieces, use fine steel wool to remove some but not all of the oxidizing solution from the surface of the fish shape, chain, clasp, and jump rings. Rinse with water, dry, and rub with polishing cloth.

11. To curve the silver fish, hold one end of the fish shape in your hand and use the chain nose pliers to hold the other end and gently curve the silver. You can also use a bracelet mandrel and rawhide mallet or a wooden baseball bat to curve the fish shape around. Set the fish shape aside.

12. Slide the silver beads and the pearl bead onto the head pin.

13. Use the ruler to measure and mark $\frac{5}{16}$" above the top bead on the head pin. With the wire cutters or tin snips, cut the head pin wire $\frac{5}{16}$" above the top bead.

14. Use the round nose pliers to bend the head pin wire next to the top bead at a 90-degree angle.

15. Hold the head pin wire with the beads on it in one hand with the wire that you bent pointing toward you. Using the round nose pliers, grip the end of the head pin wire that is pointing toward you and roll it away from you. Release the pliers from the head pin wire. You will still have an opening in the loop, so grasp the head pin wire again and roll the loop all the way closed. You can use the round nose or chain nose pliers to adjust the shape of your loop at the top of the head pin if you need to. Set this aside.

To open and close jump rings, use two pair of chain nose pliers pointing up to hold the jump ring with the opening at the top. Roll one of your wrists away from you and your other wrist toward you, opening the jump ring only as much as you need to. To close the jump ring, hold it the same way and roll your wrists in the opposite direction (think of holding a piece of paper and tearing it). Never pull the jump ring ends out, as this will weaken the metal, and it will be difficult to close the jump ring.

16. Open one oval jump ring, attach the clasp to the end links of the three 3¾" inch pieces of chain, and then close the jump ring. Next open one oval jump ring, slide it through the other end links of the 3¾" pieces of chain, and then close the jump ring. Open one oval jump ring and slide it through the hole at one end of the fish shape and then through the jump ring with the three pieces of chain attached and then close that jump ring. Open one oval jump ring and slide it through the hole in the other end of the fish shape and then close the jump ring. Attach four jump rings to the jump ring that is at the opposite end of the fish shape of the chain. Before you close the last jump ring, first slide the loop at the top of the pearl bead head pin onto the jump ring.

Hammered Sterling
Silver Fish and Chain Necklace

MATERIALS NEEDED

One 3½" 12-gauge round sterling silver wire

One 1" × 2¾" 18-gauge sterling sheet silver

Ten 5.3 × 3.2 mm sterling silver oval jump rings

One 6.5 mm 16-gauge sterling silver round
     jump ring

5" 20-gauge sterling silver wire (approximate)

Pre-made bell cap

One chunky recycled glass bead

One coral fossil

Miscellaneous fossils

Two 1¾" pieces small link sterling silver chain

Two 6½" pieces larger link sterling silver chain

One sterling silver 16 mm lobster clasp

TOOLS NEEDED

Hard, flat surface

Ball peen hammer

Marker

Jeweler's saw or tin snips

Rawhide mallet or piece of thick scrap leather

Flat hammer

File

Ruler

Fine grit sanding pad

Safety glasses

Awl

1/16" drill bit

Handheld rotary tool, flex shaft, or drill press

Liver of sulfur or oxidizing solution

Fine steel wool

Polishing cloth

Two pairs of chain nose pliers

Round nose pliers

Two-part epoxy or industrial strength glue

1. Place the ½" × 2 ½" piece of sterling sheet silver onto a hard, flat surface. (For this project, I used a regular ball peen hammer purchased at a home improvement store. There are many great jeweler's hammers available, but if you are just starting out making jewelry, you may want to start with this inexpensive version.) Use the round end of the ball peen hammer to strike the surface of the sheet silver multiple times, making a uniform hammered texture. If you will also make the earring and bracelet projects, you may want to texture all of the sterling sheet silver pieces at the same time.

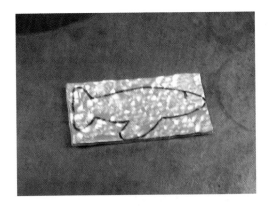

2. Decide on the shapes of the fish that you want to use and draw the shapes with marker onto the ½" × 2½" piece of 18-gauge sterling sheet silver. You can free-hand draw the fish shapes, or you can use a design from a wide selection of available clip art. You can make the fish shapes identical or make them different from each other for added interest. You may find that using a simple shape will be easier the first time you do this project.

3. Using a jeweler's saw or tin snips, cut the fish shapes from the ½" × 2 ½" hammered sterling sheet silver. If you are using tin snips and not a jeweler's saw, cut outside the marker line you drew around the fish shapes to allow you room to refine the edges with the file after the fish shapes are cut out. If you used tin snips, the pieces will not be flat after you cut them, so you will need to place the fish shapes on a hard, flat surface and use a rawhide mallet to flatten them. If you do not have a rawhide mallet, place the fish shapes on a hard, flat surface, cover the pieces with a thick piece of scrap leather, and gently tap the leather covered fish shapes with a flat hammer to flatten them.

4. The edges of the fish shapes will be sharp after you cut them out, so use a file to refine the shape of the fish and to eliminate any sharp corners or rough edges. After filing the edges, use a fine grit sanding pad to go over the area where you filed to smooth the edges and remove any file marks. Do this step to each fish shape.

5. Measure ¹⁄₁₆" from one tip of the fish shapes and place a mark where you will drill the holes (this is where you will attach them to the oval jump ring and the ½" silver chain). You can place the holes on the same end of the fish shapes, or you can place the holes so that one fish is swimming upstream and one is swimming downstream.

6. Put on the safety glasses. Place the fish shapes onto a hard, flat surface and put the point of the awl on the mark that you made ¹⁄₁₆" from the edge of the fish shape. Use a hammer to firmly strike the top of the awl once to make a pilot hole for drilling holes into the fish shapes. Set these aside.

7. Use the ruler to measure and mark the 3½" piece of 12-gauge round sterling silver wire ½" from each end of the wire. This will give you a visual guide to use when you flatten the ends of the wire with the hammer.

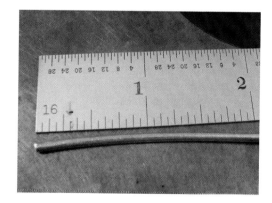

8. Lay the piece of wire onto a hard, flat surface and use a flat hammer to strike the end of the wire with a firm tap, using the ½" mark that you made on the end of the 12-gauge wire as a visual guide on where to strike the wire. You may need to strike the wire multiple times to achieve the flatness necessary to allow space to drill the holes. Do this step to both ends of the 12-gauge wire.

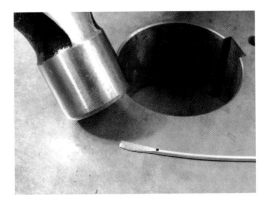

9. The ends of the 12-gauge wire will be sharp after hammering them, so use a file to eliminate any sharp or rough edges. After filing the edges, use a fine grit sanding pad to go over the area where you filed to smooth the edges and eliminate any file marks. Do this to both ends of the 12-gauge wire piece.

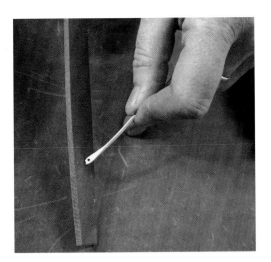

10. To curve the piece of 12-gauge wire, hold one end of the wire in the chain nose pliers and use your fingers to gently bend the wire to the desired curve.

11. Use the ruler to measure and mark ⅟₁₆" from the end of the 12-gauge wire where you flattened it. This is where you will drill the holes to attach the wire to the chain.

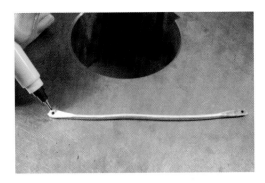

12. Put on the safety glasses. Place the 12-gauge wire onto a hard, flat surface and put the point of the awl on the mark that you made ⅟₁₆" from the end of the wire. Use a flat hammer to firmly strike the top of the awl once to make a pilot hole for drilling the holes into each end of the 12-gauge wire.

13. Using a $\frac{1}{16}$" drill bit, drill holes into each end of the curved piece of 12-gauge wire and each of the fish shapes using a handheld rotary tool, flex shaft, or drill press (don't forget to wear your safety glasses).

14. Use the ruler to measure the chain into two 1½" pieces. Use the wire cutters to cut the chain and set these pieces aside.

15. Use the file or sanding pad to eliminate any burs or rough edges left from drilling the holes into the curved piece of 12-gauge wire and the fish shapes.

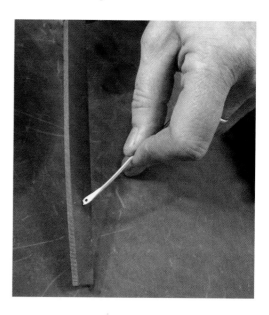

16. Apply liver of sulfur or an oxidizing solution to the fish shapes, curved piece of 12-gauge wire, piece of 20-gauge wire, chains, bell cap, clasp, and jump rings. It is very important to follow any safety recommendations the manufacturer suggests when using any chemicals.

17. After oxidizing the various pieces, use fine steel wool to remove some but not all of the oxidizing solution from the surface of the fish shapes, curved piece of 12-gauge wire, the piece of 20-gauge wire, chains, bell cap, clasp, and jump rings. Rinse with water, dry, and rub with polishing cloth.

To open and close jump rings, use two pairs of chain nose pliers pointing up to hold the jump ring with the opening at the top. Roll one of your wrists away from you and your other wrist toward you, opening the jump ring only as much as you need to. To close the jump ring, hold it the same way and roll your wrists in the opposite direction (think of holding a piece of paper and tearing it). Never pull the jump ring ends out, as this will weaken the metal, and it will be difficult to close the jump ring.

18. Open the oval jump ring, add one fish shape and one end of a ½" piece of chain, and then close the jump ring. Repeat with the other jump ring, fish shape, and chain and set these aside.

19. Use the ruler to measure and mark 1½" from the end of the 20-gauge wire. At the 1 ½" mark, use the chain nose pliers and bend the wire to a 90-degree angle. Use the round nose pliers and grasp the wire at the bend with the section that you bent pointing toward you and the longer part of the wire where the beads will be pointing down. Use your fingers to wrap the wire that is pointing toward you around the round nose pliers to form a loop. The closer that you hold the wire to the end of the jaws of the round nose pliers, the smaller the loop will be; and the farther up the jaws of the round nose pliers that you hold the wire, the larger the loop will be.

Hold the loop that you formed with the chain nose pliers and wrap the wire "tail" around the longer piece of the wire that is pointing down. When this wire has been wrapped, trim and file the end so that it will not be sharp. Use the chain nose pliers to squeeze the last loop tight against the wire. Add the beads that you have selected to the wire. Remember to allow at least 1½" of extra wire at the end of the beads.

After you add the beads to the wire, use a ruler to measure and mark 1½" above the beads. Use the wire cutters or tin snips and cut the wire at the 1½" mark. Use the ruler to measure and mark ½" above the top bead; this is where you will bend the wire at a 90-degree angle to form the wrapped loop at the other end of the beads. After bending the wire, repeat the loop and wrapping process and set this aside.

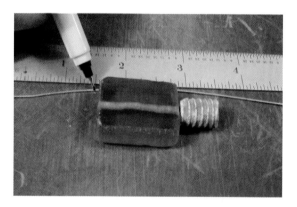

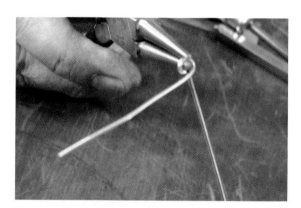

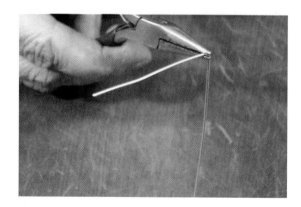

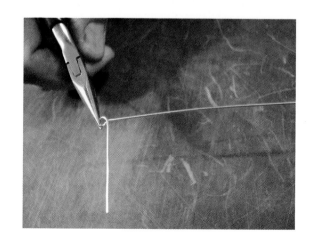

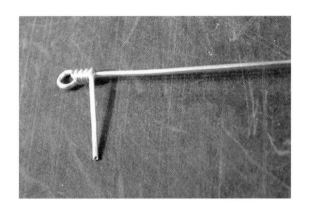

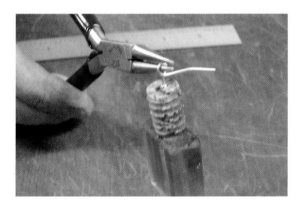

20. Attach the pre-made bell cap to the coral fossil with a two-part epoxy or industrial strength glue. Follow the directions on the adhesive and make sure that you allow the piece to dry thoroughly. Set this aside.

21. Open an oval jump ring, place it through the wrapped loop at the top of the beads, and then close the jump ring. Open another oval jump ring, place it through the wrapped loop at the bottom of the beads and the top loop of the bell cap with the coral fossil, and then close the jump ring.

22. Open an oval jump ring and attach one end of the 12-gauge curved wire to the end link of the one 6½" piece of chain, add the jump ring with the chain and fish onto the jump ring, and then close.

23. Slide the curved 12-gauge wire through the jump ring at the top of the beads.

24. Open an oval jump ring, slide it through the hole at the other end of the 12-gauge curved wire and then through the end link of the other 6½" piece of chain. Add the jump ring with the chain and fish onto the jump ring, and then close.

25. Open an oval jump ring, attach the clasp to one end link of the 6½" piece of chain, and then close the jump ring.

26. Open an oval jump ring and attach the round jump ring to the end link on the other piece of 6½" chain.

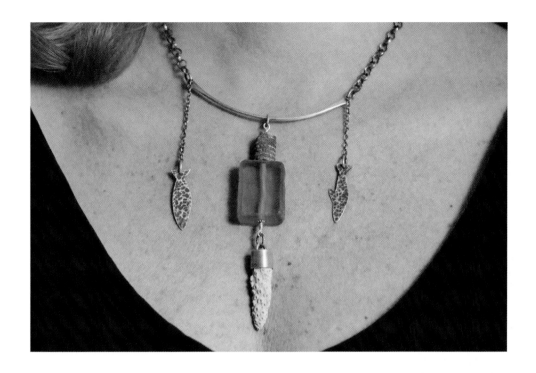

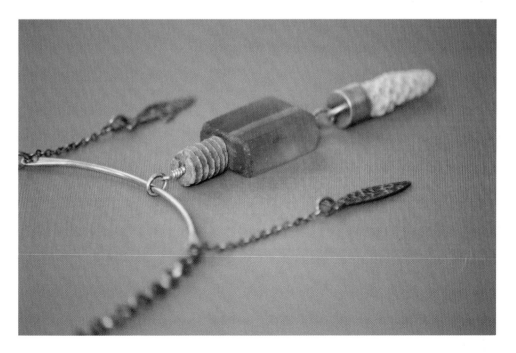

10

Classic Wrapped Loop Earrings and Necklace

Basic Loop Earrings

MATERIALS NEEDED

20-gauge sterling silver wire
Beads

TOOLS NEEDED

Ruler
Marker
Wire cutters or tin snips
Chain nose pliers
Round nose pliers
File

1. Use the ruler to measure and mark the wire at least 1½" from the end.

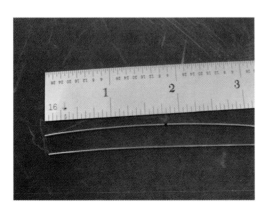

2. At the 1½" mark, use the chain nose pliers and bend the wire to a 90-degree, or right, angle.

3. Use the round nose pliers and grasp the wire at the bend with the section that you bent pointing toward you and the longer part of the wire where the beads will be pointing down.

4. Use your fingers to wrap the wire that is pointing toward you around the round nose pliers to form a loop. The closer that you hold the wire to the end of the jaws of the round nose pliers, the smaller the loop will be; and the further up the jaws of the round nose pliers that you hold the wire, the larger the loop will be.

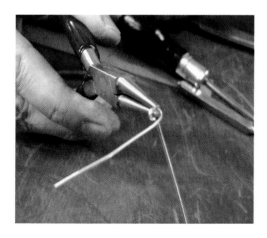

5. Hold the loop that you formed with the chain nose pliers. Wrap the wire "tail" around the longer piece of wire that is pointing down. When this wire has been wrapped, trim and file the end so that it will not be sharp.

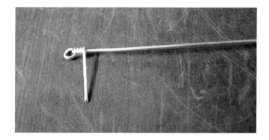

6. Use the chain nose pliers to squeeze the last loop tight against the wire. Add a bead or beads to the wire above the wrapped loop.

7. Measure at least 1½" above the top bead and cut the wire.

8. Use the ruler to measure and mark ¼" above the top bead. This is where you will bend the wire at a 90-degree angle to form the wrapped loop at the other end of the beads.

9. After bending the wire, repeat the loop and wrapping process.

Here are some examples of designs you can create with the wrapped loop technique.

Use gemstone, crystal, and sterling silver beads on a sterling silver head pin. Finish off with a wrapped loop at the top for a quick and simple but great-looking pair of earrings.

Use 20-gauge sterling silver wire, and slip the wire through a donut bead before forming the wire wrapped loop. Add a bugle bead and finish at the top with another wrapped loop.

A mixture of earth tone beads on eye pins combined with sterling silver head pins finished off with a wrapped loop.

The Wrapped Loop Necklace

Form a wrapped loop with 20-gauge sterling silver wire. Mix raku and glass beads. Form another wrapped loop at the other end. Add a jump ring to a great raku focal piece, add a jump ring to the top, and slide the whole thing onto a chain or cord.

Use 20-gauge sterling silver wire to form a spiral at one end. Use a hammer to flatten the spiral. Add glass, sterling silver, and raku beads. Finish off with a wrapped loop at the top. Add a jump ring at the top and slide onto a chain or cord.

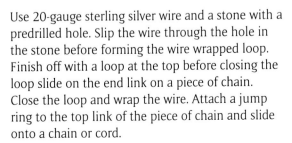

Use 20-gauge sterling silver wire and a stone with a predrilled hole. Slip the wire through the hole in the stone before forming the wire wrapped loop. Finish off with a loop at the top before closing the loop slide on the end link on a piece of chain. Close the loop and wrap the wire. Attach a jump ring to the top link of the piece of chain and slide onto a chain or cord.

Use 20-gauge sterling silver wire and assorted beads. Form a wrapped loop at each end of a wire with two beads on it. Make several of these and attach them together with jump rings. Mix it up with adding chain and sterling silver components.

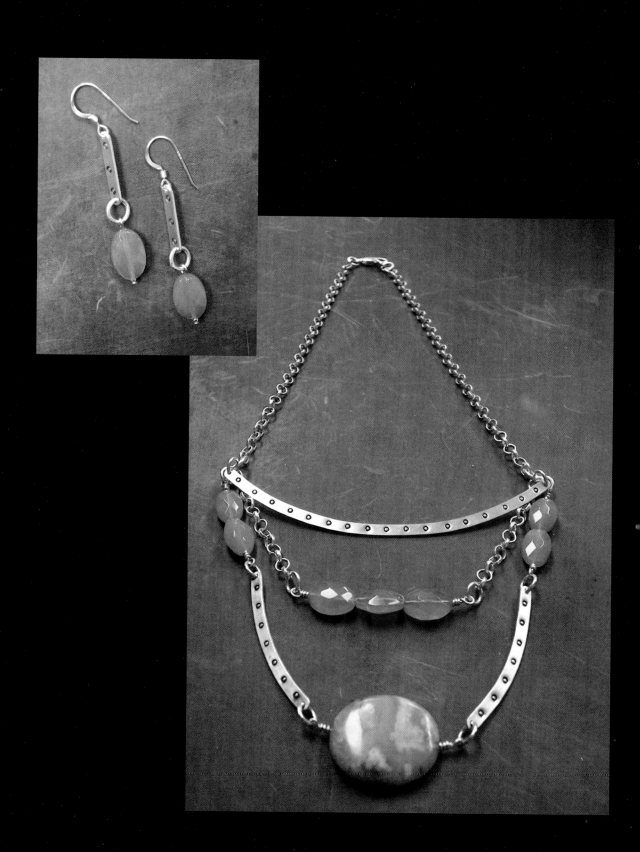

Three-Strand Sky Earrings and Necklace

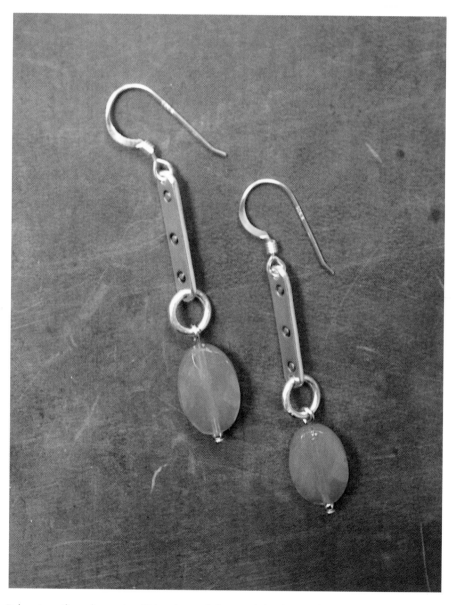

Bring together elements of the sky and the earth in these silver and sky-blue beads.

MATERIALS NEEDED

Two   14 × 10 mm flat oval beads
One   1½" 4 × 1 mm sterling silver rectangle wire
Two   1½" head pins
Two   1.4 mm round sterling silver beads
Two   5 mm 18-gauge round sterling silver jump
          rings
Two   sterling silver ear wires

TOOLS NEEDED

Ruler
Marker
Jeweler's saw or tin snips
File
Fine grit sanding pad
Safety glasses
Hard, flat surface
Awl
Hammer
Nail set punch
¹⁄₁₆" drill bit
Handheld rotary tool, flex shaft, or drill press
Liver of sulfur or oxidizing solution
Fine steel wool
Polishing cloth
Two pairs of chain nose pliers

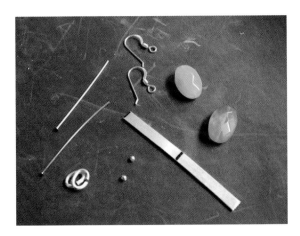

1. Use the ruler to measure and mark two ¾"
   pieces of 4 × 1 mm rectangle sterling silver
   wire.

2. Using a jeweler's saw or tin snips, cut the
   4×1 mm rectangle sterling silver wire into
   two pieces that are ¾" long.

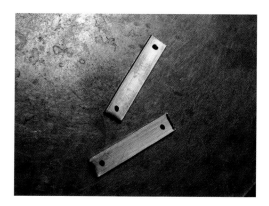

3. File each end of the ¾" rectangle wire
   pieces to remove any burs or rough edges.
   If desired, you can use the file to round the
   ends of the rectangle wire pieces. Use a fine
   grit sanding pad to go over the area you filed
   to smooth the edges and remove any file
   marks.

4. Use the ruler to measure and mark ⅟₁₆" from
   each end of the ¾" pieces of rectangle wire
   and place a mark in the center of the wire.
   This is where you will drill the holes to attach
   the jump ring and head pin with the bead
   and also the ear wire.

5. Put on your safety glasses. Place the ¾"
   rectangle wire pieces onto a hard, flat surface
   and put the point of the awl on the mark
   that you made ⅟₁₆" from each end of the
   rectangle wire. Use a hammer to firmly strike
   once on the top of the awl to make a pilot
   hole for drilling holes into each end of the
   rectangle wire.

6. Using a ¹⁄₁₆" drill bit, drill holes into each end of the rectangle wire pieces with a handheld rotary tool, flex shaft, or drill press (don't forget to wear your safety glasses).

7. Use the file or fine grit sanding pad to eliminate any burs or rough edges left from drilling holes into the rectangle wire pieces.

8. Use the ruler to measure and mark the center of each ¾" piece of rectangle wire, and then measure and mark ¼" increments up and down both of the ¾" rectangle wires. This is where you will stamp the circle shapes into the rectangle wires.

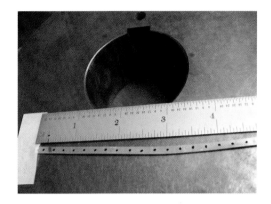

9. After marking the rectangle wires, place them onto a hard, flat surface. You can use a piece of masking tape on the ends of the rectangle wires to hold them in place while you are stamping them. Select a nail set punch. (These are inexpensive and can be purchased at any home improvement store; they usually come in sets of three sizes, mix up the sizes or choose just one size to stamp your circles.)

10. Place the nail set punch on the top of the rectangle wire where you have marked the wire and firmly strike the top of the nail set punch with the hammer to create a stamped circle shape on the rectangle wire. When you strike the top of the nail set punch, strike it only once firmly.

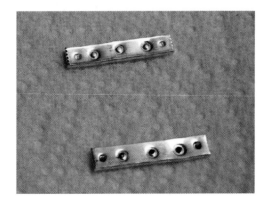

11. After stamping the circle shapes into the rectangle wire, apply liver of sulfur or oxidizing solution to the two pieces of rectangle wire. It is very important to follow any safety recommendations the manufacturer suggests when using any chemicals.

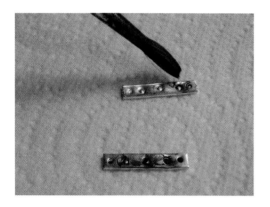

12. After using the oxidizing solution, use fine steel wool to remove the darkened area on the surface of the two pieces of rectangle wire, leaving the circles where you stamped dark. Rinse with water, dry, and rub with a polishing cloth. Set these aside.

13. Slide the 14 × 10 mm faceted flat oval bead onto a head pin.

14. Use the ruler to measure and mark $\frac{5}{16}$" above the bead on the head pin. With the wire cutters or tin snips, cut the head pin wire $\frac{5}{16}$" inch above the top bead.

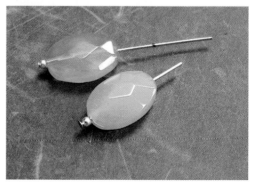

15. Use the chain nose pliers to bend the head pin wire next to the top bead at a 90-degree angle.

16. Hold the head pin with the bead on it in one hand with the wire that you bent pointing toward you. Using the round nose pliers, grip the end of the head pin wire that is pointing toward you and roll it away from you. Your hand position will be similar to that of holding a bicycle handlebar. Release the pliers from the head pin wire. Use the round nose pliers to grasp the loop of the head pin wire and roll the loop closed. You can use the round nose or chain nose pliers to adjust the shape of your loop at the top of the head pin if you want.

17. Repeat these steps for the second head pin and bead.

To open and close jump rings, use two pair of chain nose pliers pointing up to hold the jump ring with the opening at the top. Roll one of your wrists away from you and your other wrist toward you, opening the jump ring only as much as you need to. To close the jump ring, hold it the same way and roll your wrists in the opposite direction (think of holding a piece of paper and tearing it). Never pull the jump ring ends out, as this will weaken the metal and it will be difficult to close the jump ring.

18. Using two pairs of chain nose pliers, open a jump ring and attach the loop of the head pin with the bead to one end of the stamped rectangle wire. Repeat this with the other head pin with the bead and rectangle wire.

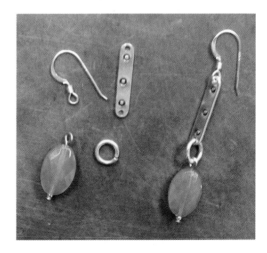

19. With chain nose pliers gently open the loop at the bottom of the ear wire and add the other end of the rectangle wire. Close the ear wire loop. Repeat with the second earring.

MATERIALS NEEDED

9" 4 × 1 mm sterling silver rectangle wire

Seven 14 × 10mm flat oval beads

One 30 × 25 × 5 mm flat oval bead

15" 20-gauge sterling silver wire (approximate)

15" of chain

Fifteen 5 mm 18-gauge round sterling silver jump rings

Three 6 mm 14-gauge round sterling silver jump rings

One 16 mm sterling silver lobster clasp

TOOLS NEEDED

Ruler

Marker

Jeweler's saw or tin snips

File

Fine grit sanding pad

Safety glasses

Hard, flat surface

Awl

Hammer

Nail set punch

$\frac{1}{16}$" drill bit

Handheld rotary tool, flex shaft, or drill press

Liver of sulfur or oxidizing solution

Fine steel wool

Polishing cloth

Two pairs of chain nose pliers

1. Use the ruler to measure and mark one 5" and two 2" pieces of 4 × 1 mm rectangle sterling silver wire.

2. Using a jeweler's saw or tin snips, cut the 4 × 1 mm rectangle sterling silver wire into one 5" and two 2" lengths.

3. File each end of the 5" and 2" rectangle wire pieces to remove any burs or rough edges. If desired, you can use the file to round the ends of the rectangle wire pieces. Use a fine grit sanding pad to go over the area you filed to smooth the edges and remove any file marks.

4. Use the ruler to measure and mark ¹⁄₁₆" from each end of the 5" and 2" pieces of rectangle wire and place a mark in the center of the wire. This will be where you will drill the holes to attach the rectangle wire pieces to the chain and wire wrapped loop beads.

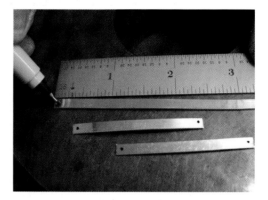

5. Put on your safety glasses. Place the 5" and 2" rectangle wire pieces onto a hard, flat surface and put the point of the awl on the mark that you made ¹⁄₁₆" from each end of the rectangle wire. Firmly strike once on the top of the awl with a hammer to make a pilot hole for drilling holes into the rectangle wire.

6. Using a ¹⁄₁₆" drill bit, drill holes into each end of the rectangle wire pieces with a handheld rotary tool, flex shaft, or drill press (don't forget to wear your safety glasses).

7. Use the file or fine grit sanding pad to eliminate any burs or rough edges left from drilling holes into the rectangle wire pieces.

8. Use the ruler to measure and mark the center of the 5" and 2" pieces of rectangle wire and then mark ¼" increments up and down all three pieces of rectangle wire. This is where you will stamp the circle shapes into the rectangle wires.

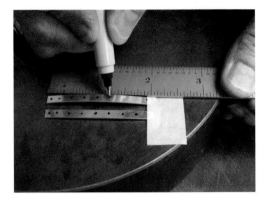

9. After marking the rectangle wires, place them onto a hard, flat surface. You can use a piece of masking tape on the ends of the rectangle wires to hold them in place while you stamp them. Select a nail set punch (these are inexpensive and can be purchased at any home improvement store. They usually come in sets of three sizes; mix up the sizes or choose just one size to stamp your circles).

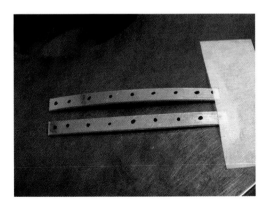

10. Place the nail set punch on the top of the rectangle wire and firmly strike the top of the nail set punch with the hammer to create a stamped circle shape on the rectangle wire. When you strike the top of the nail set punch, strike it only once firmly. Do this to all of the ¼" marks that you made on the three pieces of rectangle wire.

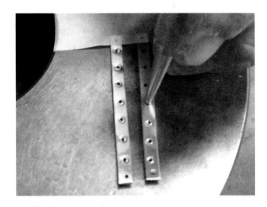

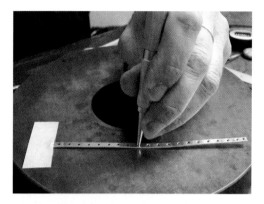

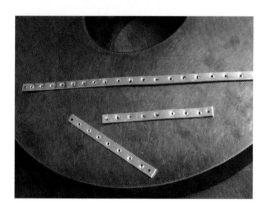

11. Apply liver of sulfur or oxidizing solution to the three pieces of rectangle wire. It is very important to follow any safety recommendations the manufacturer suggests when using any chemicals.

12. After using the oxidizing solution, use fine steel wool to remove the darkened area on the surface of the three pieces of rectangle wire, leaving the circles where you stamped dark. Rinse with water, dry, and rub with a polishing cloth.

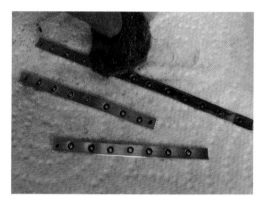

13. To curve the rectangle wire pieces, you can use a bracelet mandrel and rawhide mallet, use your hand and curve them around a baseball bat or wooden dowel, or use two pair of chain nose pliers and gently coax the rectangle wire pieces into the desired curves. Set these aside.

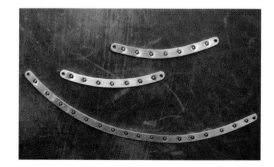

14. Use the ruler to measure and mark the 20-gauge sterling silver wire 1½" from the end. At the 1½" mark, use the chain nose pliers and bend the wire to a 90-degree angle. Use the round nose pliers and grasp the wire at the bend with the section that you bent pointing toward you and the longer part of the wire where the beads will be pointing down. Use your fingers to wrap the wire that is pointing toward you around the round nose pliers to form a loop. The closer that you hold the wire to the end of the jaws of the round nose pliers, the smaller the loop will be; the farther up the jaws of the round nose pliers that you hold the wire, the larger the loop will be. Hold the loop that that you formed with the chain nose pliers and wrap the wire "tail" around the longer piece of wire that is pointing down. When this wire has been wrapped, trim and file the end so that it will not be sharp. Use the chain nose pliers to squeeze the last loop tight against the wire. Add two 14 × 10 mm faceted flat oval beads to the wire above the wrapped loop. Measure at least 1½" above the top bead and cut the wire. Use the ruler to measure and mark approximately ¼" above the top bead; this is where you will bend the wire at a 90-degree angle to form the wrapped loop at the other end of the beads. After bending the wire, repeat the loop and wrapping process.

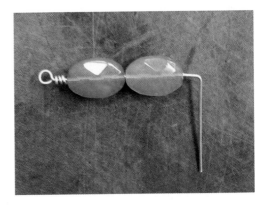

15. Repeat this step using two 14×10 mm faceted flat oval beads, repeat this step using three 14×10 mm faceted flat oval beads, and then repeat this step on the 30×25×5 mm flat oval bead.

16. To connect all of the components, start at the bottom of the necklace and work up.

To open and close jump rings, use two pair of chain nose pliers pointing up to hold the jump ring with the opening at the top. Roll one of your wrists away from you and your other wrist toward you, opening the jump ring only as much as you need to. To close the jump ring, hold it the same way and roll your wrists in the opposite direction (think of holding a piece of paper and tearing it). Never pull the jump ring ends out, as this will weaken the metal, and it will be difficult to close the jump ring.

17. Using 5 mm 18-gauge jump rings, connect the two 14×10 mm faceted flat oval wrapped loop beads to one end of a 2" piece of rectangle wire. Use a 5 mm 18-gauge jump ring to connect the 2" piece of rectangle wire to the 30×25×5 mm flat oval wrapped loop bead. On the other side of the flat oval bead, connect the other 2" piece of rectangle wire and the other two faceted flat oval wrapped loop beads. Set these aside.

18. Measure and cut two 2" pieces of chain. Using 5 mm 18-gauge jump rings, attach a 2" piece of chain to each side of the three faceted flat oval wrapped loop beads. Set these aside.

19. Measure and cut two 6½" pieces of chain. Use a 5 mm 18-gauge jump ring to connect the 16 mm sterling silver lobster clasp to one end of a 6½" piece of chain. Add three 5 mm 18-gauge and one 6 mm 14-gauge jump rings to one end of the other piece of 6½" piece of chain. Go ahead and open the lobster clasp and connect it to the end jump ring on the other piece of chain. This will make it easier to assemble the remainder of the necklace.

20. Lay the necklace components onto a flat surface in the order that you will be assembling them. Use a 5 mm 18-gauge jump ring to attach the end of a wrapped loop, the end of a 2" piece of chain, and one end of a 5" piece of curved rectangle wire. Repeat this step on the other side.

21. Use the 6 mm 14-gauge jump rings to attach the jump ring connecting the three necklace strands together to the end link of a 6½" piece of chain. Repeat this step on the other side.

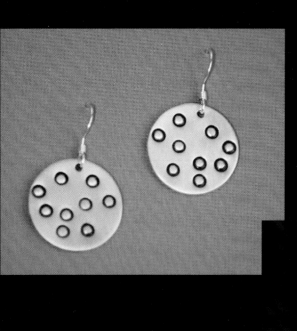

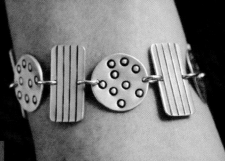

Fun Variations— Combining Components

Sterling Silver Stamped Disc Earrings

Combine all the techniques you've learned to create these one-of-a-kind pieces.

MATERIALS NEEDED

Two ¾" 18-gauge sterling silver discs cut from
    sheet silver
Two sterling silver ear wires

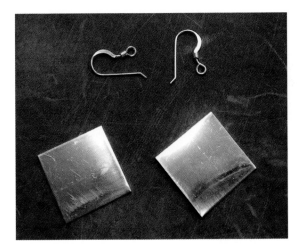

TOOLS NEEDED

Jeweler's saw or tip snips
Marker
Penny
Chain nose pliers
File
Fine grit sanding pad
Hard, flat surface
Scissors
Masking tape
Nail set punch
Hammer
Ruler
Safety glasses
Awl
1/16" drill bit
Handheld rotary tool, flex shaft, or drill press
Liver of sulfur or oxidizing solution
Fine steel wool
Polishing cloth

1. To cut ¾" 18-gauge sterling silver discs from the sheet silver, use a marker to draw around a penny. This will give you the ¾" size needed for this project. Use a jeweler's saw or tin snips to cut around the outside of the marker line. This will allow you room to refine the edges with the file once all your discs are cut. If using tin snips to cut, allow extra space between the discs when drawing around the penny so you will be able to cut more easily. It may be easier to cut the sheet silver into squares then round the edges when cutting.

2. Once you have cut the two discs from the sheet silver, use a file to refine the shape of the discs and to eliminate any rough edges. You can use the marker line you had drawn around the penny to guide you. Once you have filed the edges and gotten the disc shape, use a fine grit sanding pad to go over the area where you have filed to smooth the edges and remove any file marks. Do this step to both discs.

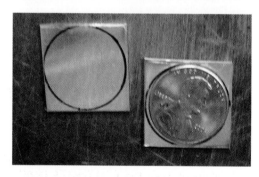

3. Place the discs onto a hard, flat surface. You can use masking tape on the edges of the discs to keep them in place while you are stamping them. Select a nail set punch. These are inexpensive and can be purchased at any home improvement store. They usually come in sets of three sizes. Mix up the sizes or choose just one size to stamp your circles.

4. Place the nail set punch on the top of the disc and with the hammer firmly strike the top of the nail set punch to create a stamped circle shape on the disc. Do this randomly over the surface of the discs approximately seven to nine times. If desired, you can mark the discs where you want to stamp them before you begin. When you strike the top of the nail set punch, strike it only once firmly. If you strike the top of the nail set punch multiple times, the punch may skip across the silver and scratch the surface of the discs.

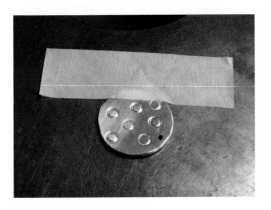

5. This process may leave your discs misshapen or with sharp edges, so after you have stamped the nail set punch circles into all three discs, check the edges to see if you need to refile the edges to regain the circular shape and eliminate any sharp edges. After filing, use a fine grit sanding pad to go over the area you have filed to smooth the edges and remove any file marks. The silver discs will have a slight curve to them. You can leave the silver discs curved, or you can flatten them. Simply place the silver discs onto a hard, flat surface and use a rawhide mallet to flatten them. If you do not have a rawhide mallet, you can place the silver discs on a hard, flat surface and cover the pieces with a thick piece of scrap leather; then, with a hammer, gently tap the leather-covered silver discs to flatten them.

6. Lay out your stamped discs to determine where you would like the holes to be drilled. Use the ruler to measure and mark $1/16$" from the edge of the discs. This is where the holes are to be drilled.

7. Put on safety glasses. Place the discs onto a hard, flat surface. Place the point of the awl on the mark that you made $1/16$" from the edge of the discs and, using a hammer, firmly strike the top of the awl once to make a pilot hole for drilling holes into the discs.

8. Using a $1/16$" drill bit, drill holes into each of the discs using a handheld rotary tool, flex shaft, or drill press. Wear safety glasses!

9. Use the file or fine sanding pad to eliminate any burs or rough edges left from drilling holes into the discs.

10. Apply liver of sulfur or oxidizing solution to the discs. It is very important to follow any safety recommendations the manufacturer suggests on the directions when using any chemicals.

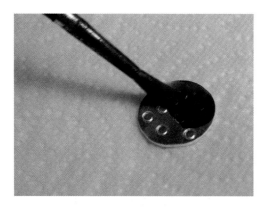

11. After following the oxidizing instructions, use fine steel wool to remove the darkened area on the surface of the discs, leaving the circles where you stamped dark. Rinse with water, dry, and rub with a polishing cloth.

12. With chain nose pliers, gently open the loop at the bottom of the ear wire and add the disc. Close the ear wire loop.

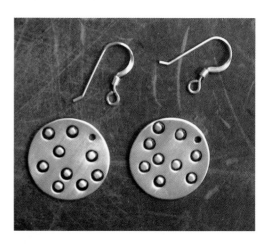

13. Repeat with other earring.

Stamped Sterling Silver Disc Necklace

MATERIALS NEEDED

Three ¾" 18-gauge sterling silver discs cut from sheet

Four 16-gauge 5.3 × 3.2 sterling silver oval jump rings

One sterling silver chain with clasp

TOOLS NEEDED

Jeweler's saw or tip snips
Marker
Penny
File
Fine grit sanding pad
Hard, flat surface
Scissors
Masking tape
Nail set punch
Hammer
Ruler
Safety glasses
Awl
1/16" drill bit
Handheld rotary tool, flex shaft, or drill press
Liver of sulfur or oxidizing solution
Fine steel wool
Polishing cloth
Two pairs of chain nose pliers

1. To cut ¾" 18-gauge sterling silver discs from the sheet silver, use a marker to draw around a penny. This will give you the ¾" size needed for this project. Use a jeweler's saw or tin snips to cut around the outside of the marker line. This will allow you room to refine the edges with the file once all your discs are cut. If using tin snips to cut, allow extra space between the discs when drawing around the penny so you will be able to cut more easily. It may be easier to cut the sheet silver into squares then round the edges when cutting.

2. Once you have cut the three discs from the sheet silver, use a file to refine the shape of the discs and to eliminate any rough edges. You can use the mark you had drawn around the penny to guide you. Once you have filed the edges and gotten the disc shape, use a fine grit sanding pad to go over the area where you filed to smooth the edges and remove any file marks. Do this to all three discs.

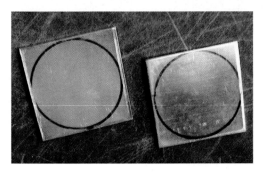

3. Place the discs onto a hard, flat surface. You can use masking tape on the edges of the discs to keep them in place while you are stamping them. Select a nail set punch. These are inexpensive and can be purchased at any home improvement store. They usually come in sets of three sizes; mix up the sizes or choose just one size to stamp the discs.

4. Place the nail set punch on the top of the discs and, with the hammer, gently strike the top of the nail set punch to create a stamped circle shape on the discs. Do this randomly over the surface of the discs approximately seven to nine times. If desired, you can mark the discs where you want to stamp them before you begin. When you strike the top of the nail set punch, strike it only once firmly. If you strike the top of the nail set punch multiple times, the punch may skip across the silver and scratch the surface of the discs.

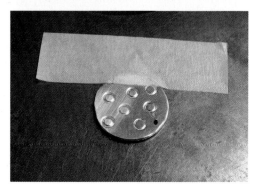

5. This process may leave your discs misshapen or with sharp edges, so after you have stamped the nail set punch circles into all three discs, check the edges to see if you need to refile them to regain the circular shape and eliminate any sharp edges. After filing, use a fine grit sanding pad to go over the area you have filed to smooth the edges and remove any file marks. The silver discs will have a slight curve to them. You can leave the silver discs curved or flatten them. Simply place the silver discs onto a hard flat surface and use a rawhide mallet to flatten them. If you do not have a rawhide mallet you can place the silver discs onto a hard, flat surface and cover the pieces with a thick piece of scrap leather. With a hammer, gently tap the leather-covered silver discs to flatten them.

6. Lay out your stamped discs to determine where you would like the holes to be drilled. Use the ruler to measure and mark $1/16$" from the edge of the discs; this is where the holes will be drilled.

7. Put on safety glasses. Place the discs onto a hard, flat surface. Place the point of the awl on the marks that you made $1/16$" from the edge of the discs and, using a hammer, firmly strike the top of the awl once to make a pilot hole for drilling holes into the sterling silver discs.

8. Using a $1/16$" drill bit, drill holes into each of the discs using a handheld rotary tool, flex shaft, or drill press. Wear safety glasses!

9. Use the file or fine sanding pad to eliminate any burs or rough edges left from drilling holes into the discs.

10. Apply liver of sulfur or oxidizing solution to the discs. It is very important to follow any safety recommendations the manufacturer suggests on the directions when using any chemicals.

To open and close jump rings, with two pair of chain nose pliers pointing up, hold the jump ring with the opening at the top. Roll one of your wrists away from you and your other wrist towards you. Opening the jump ring only as much as needed. To close the jump ring; hold it the same way and roll your wrists in the opposite direction. Think of holding a piece of paper and tearing it! Never pull the jump rings out, this will weaken the metal, and it will be difficult to close the jump ring.

11. After following the oxidizing instructions, use fine steel wool to remove the darkened area on the surface of the discs, leaving the circles that you stamped dark. Rinse with water, dry, and rub with a polishing cloth.

12. Using two pair of chain nose pliers, attach one disc to the center of the chain using one jump ring.

13. To evenly space the discs on the chain, you can count the links of chain between where you attach the discs. Use jump rings to attach the other two discs to the chain.

Sterling Silver Stamped Disc and Rectangles Bracelet

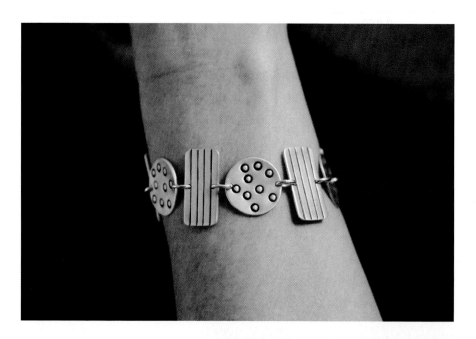

MATERIALS NEEDED

Five ¾" 18-gauge sterling silver discs cut from
sheet silver

Four ½" × 1" 18-gauge sterling silver rectangles

Fourteen 16-gauge 5.3 × 3.2 sterling silver oval
jump rings

One 14-gauge 6 mm sterling silver round jump ring

One 16 mm sterling silver lobster clasp

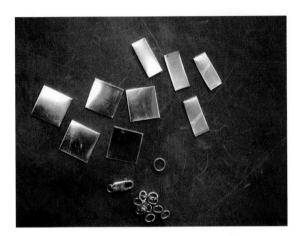

TOOLS NEEDED

Ruler
Marker
Jeweler's saw or tip snips
Four pieces of 20-gauge floral wire
Scissors
Masking tape
Tweezers
Hard, flat surface
Hammer
Safety glasses
File
fine grit sanding pad
penny
Nail set punch
Awl
⅟₁₆" drill bit
Handheld rotary tool, flex shaft, or drill press
Liver of sulfur or oxidizing solution
Fine steel wool
Polishing cloth
Two pairs of chain nose pliers

1. Use the ruler to measure and mark four ½" × 1" rectangles on the 18-gauge sheet silver. Using a jeweler's saw or tin snips, cut the rectangles from the sheet silver. Set these aside.

2. Use the ruler to measure and mark the floral wire to 1½" pieces. With the tin snips, cut the floral wire into 16 pieces approximately 1½" long.

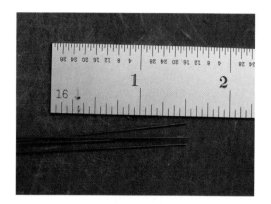

3. Cut a piece of masking tape approximately 2" long and place four of the 1½"-long pieces of floral wire onto the sticky side of the tape. Using tweezers will help with placement of the floral wire parallel onto to the sticky side of the tape

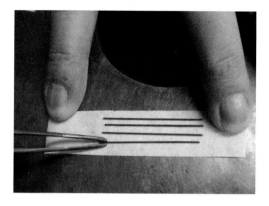

4. Place the piece of tape with the floral wire on top of a ½" × 1" silver rectangle.

5. Place the piece of tape with the floral wire and the silver rectangle pieces onto a hard, flat surface with the silver on the bottom. This will help keep the floral wire and silver rectangle piece in place while you are hammering them.

6. Put on safety glasses. With a hammer, gently strike the tape-covered silver rectangle pieces. The tape will darken where you have made contact with the floral wire. You will be trying to achieve a uniform darkness over the floral wire area. When you strike the top of the tape, use a firm strike; you do not want to hit too hard. You can achieve the desired texture more easily with many soft strikes rather than fewer harder strikes. When the tape has darkened where the floral wire is, gently lift the tape and floral wire off of the silver rectangle, and you will see indentations made from the floral wire.

7. After you complete this process with all of the rectangles, their edges will be misshapen and sharp. Use the file to eliminate any sharp corners and rough edges. After filing, use a fine grit sanding pad to go over the area where you filed to smooth the edges and remove any file marks. Set the rectangle pieces aside.

8. To cut ¾" 18-gauge sterling silver discs from the sheet silver, use a marker to draw around a penny. This will give you the ¾" size needed for this project. Use a jeweler's saw or tin snips to cut around the outside of the marker line. This will allow you room to refine the edges with the file once all your discs are cut. If using tin snips to cut, allow extra space between the discs when drawing around the penny so you will be able to cut easier. It may be easier to cut the sheet silver into squares then round the edges when cutting.

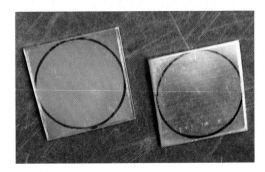

9. Once you have cut the five discs from the sheet silver, use a file to refine the shape of the discs and to eliminate any rough edges. You can use the marker line you had drawn around the penny to guide you. Once you have filed the edges and gotten the disc shape, use a fine grit sanding pad to go over the area where you have filed to smooth the edges and remove any file marks. Do this to all five discs.

10. Place the discs onto a hard, flat surface. You can use masking tape on the edges of the discs to keep them in place while you are stamping them. Select a nail set punch. These are inexpensive and can be purchased at any home improvement store. They usually come in sets of three sizes; mix up the sizes or choose just one size to stamp your discs.

11. Place the nail set punch on top of the discs and with the hammer firmly strike the top of the nail set punch to create a stamped circle shape on the disc. Do this randomly over the surface of the discs approximately seven to nine times. If desired, you can mark the discs where you want to stamp them before you begin. When you strike the top of the nail set punch, strike it only once firmly. If you strike the top of the nail set punch multiple times, the punch may skip across the silver and scratch the surface of the discs.

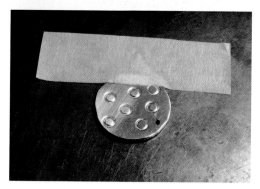

12. This process may leave your discs misshapen or with sharp edges, so after you have stamped the nail set punch circles into all five discs, check the edges to see if you need to refile the edges to regain the circular shape and eliminate any sharp edges. After filing, use a fine grit sanding pad to go over the area you have filed to smooth the edges and remove any file marks.

13. Lay out your stamped discs and stamped rectangles to determine where you would like the holes to be drilled to connect them. Use the ruler to measure and mark $\frac{1}{16}$" from each edge of the discs and rectangles; this is where the holes are to be drilled.

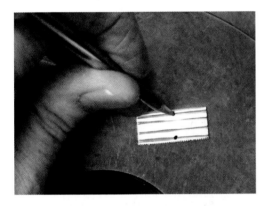

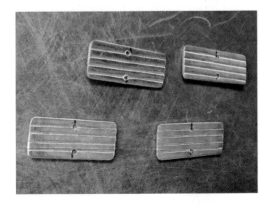

14. Put on safety glasses. Place the discs and rectangles onto a hard, flat surface. Place the point of the awl on the mark that you made $\frac{1}{16}$" from the edge of the discs and rectangles and, using a hammer, firmly strike the top of the awl once to make a pilot hole, this is where the holes are to be drilled.

15. Using a $\frac{1}{16}$" drill bit, drill holes into each of the discs and rectangles using a handheld rotary tool, flex shaft, or drill press. Wear safety glasses!

16. Use the file or fine sanding pad to eliminate any burs or rough edges left from drilling holes into the discs and rectangles.

17. Apply liver of sulfur or oxidizing solution to the discs and rectangles. It is very important to follow any safety recommendations the manufacturer suggests on the directions when using any chemicals.

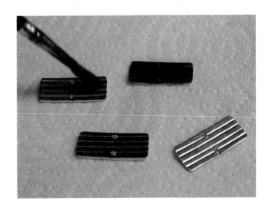

18. After following the oxidizing instructions, use fine steel wool to remove the darkened area on the surface of the discs and rectangles, leaving the areas where you stamped dark. Rinse with water, dry, and rub with a polishing cloth.

19. Lay the discs and rectangles into the order that is pleasing to you and begin to assemble them with the jump rings.

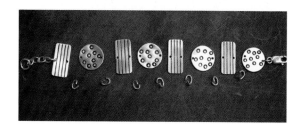

20. Using two pairs of chain nose pliers, attach clasp to disc with jump ring, attach disc to rectangle with jump ring.

Alternate...

Disc
jump ring
rectangle
jump ring
disc
jump ring
rectangle
jump ring
disc
jump ring
rectangle
jump ring
disc

When you have the clasp, five discs, and four rectangles attached together, add four jump rings and one 14-gauge 16 mm round jump ring to the end of the bracelet.

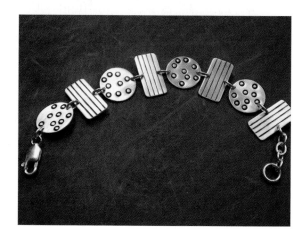

Spiral Component

MATERIALS NEEDED

4" 4 × 1 mm sterling silver rectangle wire
Two 1" head pins

TOOLS NEEDED

Ruler
Marker
Jeweler's saw or tin snips
Awl
Hammer
Hard, flat surface
$\frac{1}{16}$" drill bit
Handheld rotary tool, flex shaft, or drill press
File
Fine sanding pad
Wire cutters or tin snips
Round nose pliers
Chain nose pliers

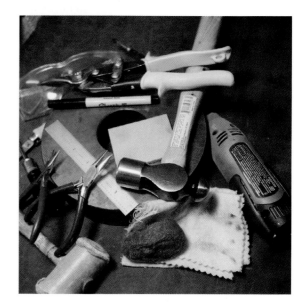

1. Use a ruler to measure and mark one 4"
   4 × 1 mm sterling silver rectangle wire.
   Use the jeweler's saw or tin snips to cut the
   4 × 1 mm sterling silver wire to 4".

2. File each end of the 4" rectangle wire piece
   to remove any burs or rough edges. If
   desired, you can use the file to round the
   ends of the rectangle wire pieces. Use a fine
   grit sanding pad to go over the area where
   you have filed to smooth the edges and
   remove any file marks.

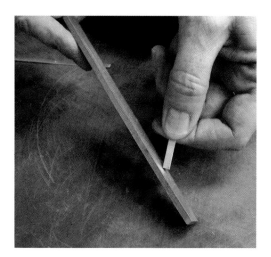

3. Use the ruler to measure and place a mark
   in the center of the wire ¾" from one end of
   the wire. Use the ruler to measure and place
   a mark in the center of the wire 2" from the
   same end of the wire. This is where you will
   be drilling holes to slide the head pins
   through.

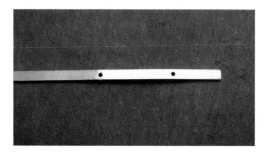

4. Put on your safety glasses. Place the 4"
   rectangle wire piece onto a hard, flat surface.
   Place the point of the awl on the mark that
   you made ¾" and 2" from the end of the
   rectangle wire, and, using a hammer, firmly
   strike once on the top of the awl. This will
   make pilot holes for drilling holes into the
   rectangle wire.

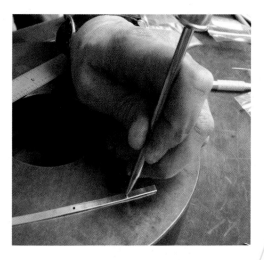

5. Using a ¹⁄₁₆" drill bit, drill holes into the
   rectangle wire piece with a handheld rotary
   tool, flex shaft, or drill press. (Wearing your
   safety glasses!)

6. Use the file or fine grit sanding pad to
   eliminate any burs or rough edges left f
   drilling holes into the rectangle wire p

7. Use the round nose pliers to grasp the end of the rectangle wire at the opposite end of the wire from where the holes were drilled. Hold the end of the rectangle wire in the jaws of the round nose pliers and, with your other hand, bend the rectangle wire around the pliers forming the spiral. When you are bending the area of the rectangle wire where you have drilled the holes, the wire will bend more easily than where no holes have been drilled. Use caution when bending the rectangle wire in that area. You may want to use a pair of chain nose pliers to hold the rectangle wire where the holes have been drilled. When you have formed the spiral, the holes that were drilled into the rectangle wire should be on opposite sides of the spiral.

8. Place a head pin through the hole drilled into one side of the rectangle wire spiral with the bottom or flat end on the inside curve of the rectangle wire spiral. Use the ruler to measure and mark the head pin $5/16"$ above the rectangle wire. With wire cutters or tin snips, cut the head pin wire $5/16"$ above the top of the rectangle wire.

9. Using the chain nose pliers, bend the head pin wire next to the rectangle wire at a 90-degree angle.

10. With chain nose pliers in one hand, hold the bottom or flat area of the head pin firmly against the rectangle wire with the head pin wire that you bent pointing toward you. With your other hand, use the round nose pliers to grip the end of the head pin wire and roll away from you. Release the head pin wire. Grasp the loop again with the round nose pliers and roll it closed. If needed, you can use the round nose or chain nose pliers to adjust the shape of the loop at the top of the head pin.

11. Repeat this step using the other head pin to slide through the hole on the other side of the rectangle wire spiral.

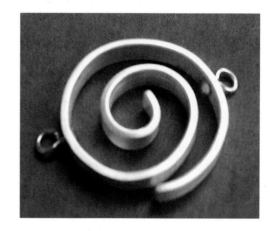

Hippie Queen Bracelet

Components used in the next two projects are derived from several other projects demonstrated earlier in this book.

Here is the order in which to assemble the components:

Clasp
Jump ring
Stamped rectangle
Jump ring
Gold bead wrapped loop
Jump ring
Spiral
Jump ring
Blue wrapped loop bead
Jump ring
Stamped disc
Five jump rings
One large jump ring with orange bead on a head pin

Long Hippie Queen Necklace

Left side of long necklace
Orange bead-wrapped loop

Jump ring

Spiral-sterling silver rectangle wire

Jump ring

Gold bead-wrapped loop

Jump ring

Chain—three links of sterling silver

Jump ring

Rectangle sterling silver

Jump ring

Green bead, blue bead, wrapped loop

Jump ring

Disc-stamped sterling silver

Jump ring

Spiral-sterling silver rectangle wire

Jump ring

Chain—two links of sterling silver

Jump ring

Disc-stamped sterling silver

Right side of long necklace
Orange bead-wrapped loop

Jump ring

Rectangle-stamped sterling silver

Jump ring

Green bead-wrapped loop

Jump ring

Chain—two links of sterling silver

Jump ring

Disc-stamped sterling silver

Jump ring

Blue bead, orange bead, wrapped loop

Jump ring

Rectangle-stamped sterling silver

Jump ring

Chain—three links of sterling silver

Jump ring

Gold bead-wrapped loop

jump ring

clasp 16mm sterling silver lobster

Connect at the top of the sides using jump rings and two links of chain.

Resources

Sources for Tools and Materials

Laura Villianyi
LAURA-WORLD.com
Handmade glass beads

Rachael Schatko and Ingrid Craft of raku beads
coalcreekclay@sbcglobal.com

Beadforlife.org
Handmade beads

Spencer Lapidary
spencerlapidary.com
Fossils

Rio Grande
riogrande.com
Tools, materials, and findings. They include great tips and information on the items that they carry.

Fire Mountain Gems and Beads
firemountiangems.com
Assorted beads and findings; also include great tips and information on the items that they carry.

Visit craft and hobby retailers like Michael's, Hobby Lobby, and others who carry jewelry materials and supplies.

Periodicals

Lapidary Journal Jewelry Arts
jewelryartistmagazine.com
Along with lots of information, they publish an annual buyer's guide issue.

Art Jewelry-magazine
ArtJewelryMag.com

Books

The Complete Metalsmith: An Illustrated Handbook, by Tim McCreight, published 1982, ISBN 0871921359. This is Denise's favorite, and the first jewelry instruction book she ever purchased. It has been with her from the beginning. It is well worn and much used and is always within arm's reach. Newer versions of this book have been published, one in 1991, and others even more recently, but this is the one Denise uses every day.

Many other books are available for all experience levels. Look through several and decide which form of instruction fits you best. Referral from other jewelry makers, or word of mouth, is also a good way to find books. You can pick up tips and ideas in every book you read, so all have merit.

Web Sites

Ganoskin.com

About.com/jewelrymaking

Contacting the Author

Contact Denise through her web site, de@detchisonjewelry.com, or at detchstudio@yahoo.com.

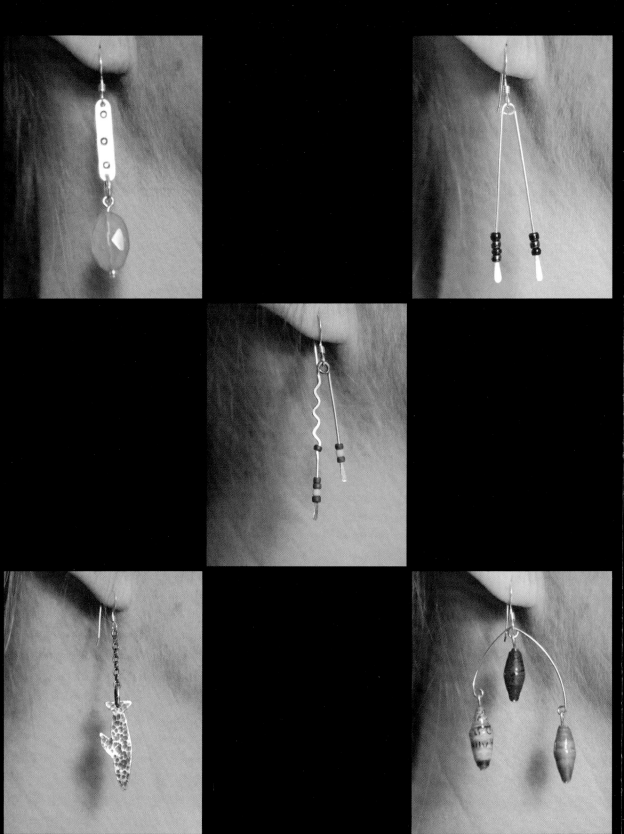

Index

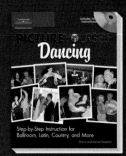

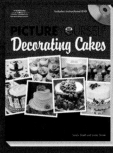

NOTES

NOTES

NOTES